W9-AHH-595

Tattoos and Body Piercing

by Leanne K. Currie-McGhee

LUCENT Overview Series

LUCENT BOOKS
An imprint of Thomson Gale, a part of The Thomson Corporation

THOMSON
★
™
GALE

Detroit • New York • San Francisco • San Diego • New Haven, Conn. • Waterville, Maine • London • Munich

LIBRARY OF CONGRESS CATALOGING-IN-PUBLICATION DATA
Currie-McGhee, L. K. (Leanne K.)
Tattoos and body piercing / by Leanne K. Currie-McGhee.
p. cm. — (Overview series)
Includes bibliographical references and index.
ISBN 1-59018-749-0 (hard cover : alk. paper)
1. Tattooing—Juvenile literature. 2. Body piercing—Juvenile literature. 3. Body marking—Juvenile literature. I. Title. II. Lucent overview series.
GT2345.C87 2005
391.6'5—dc22
2005004761

Printed in the United States of America

Contents

Introduction

IN THE PAST three decades, body piercing and tattooing have become increasingly popular among Americans from all walks of life and of all ages. For example, Kathryn, a seventy-five-year-old woman, recently decided to get a tattoo while vacationing in Hawaii. She picked a small rose because it symbolizes her hometown of Portland, Oregon, known as the "City of Roses." Kathryn had the rose tattooed on her ankle.

Just fifty years ago, most Americans would have considered Kathryn's act an unconventional activity practiced only by rebels such as prisoners and bikers. However, today many people accept tattooing and piercing as fashionable ways to decorate the body. Most of Kathryn's friends complimented her on her tattoo. "When I got back home," she said, "everybody at my retirement complex thought it was absolutely fantastic! Except for one person; she thought it was just horrible."[1]

Body Art Origins

Although tattooing and body piercing may seem like recent trends, the practice of getting permanent body art actually dates back to prehistoric times. Tattooed mummies have been found all over the world, from central Asia to western Europe. The oldest tattooed mummy was discovered in the Otztaler Alps between Austria and Italy and is estimated to be fifty-three hundred years old. This mummy had a tattooed band of stripes on his lower back, a cross behind his left knee, and more stripes on his ankle. Prehistoric people practiced tattooing by puncturing the skin with crude tools dipped in pigment.

Evidence also shows that people pierced their bodies thousands of years ago. Archaeologists discovered a five-thousand-year-old female figurine from Iran with multiple ear piercings. Another piece of evidence was found in Cyprus. There, archaeologists discovered a pair of gold earrings more than twenty-two hundred years old.

People all over the world practiced tattooing and body piercing. Tattooing was a common practice among tribes in the Pacific Islands. For example, the Maori of New Zealand decorated their faces with tattoos, and Samoan men tattooed areas from their waist to just below the knees. In

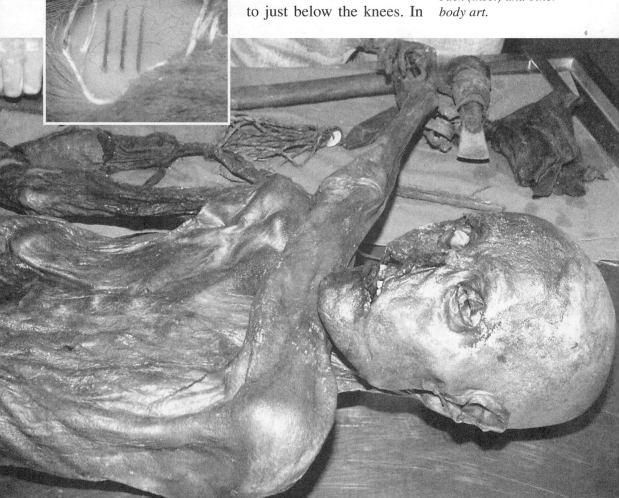

Scientists studying Otzi, the five-thousand-year-old mummy found in the Otztaler Alps, discovered a tattoo of vertical stripes on his back (inset) and other body art.

The face and shoulders of this Maori man are heavily ornamented with tribal motifs. Historically, tattooing was a very common practice in the Pacific Islands.

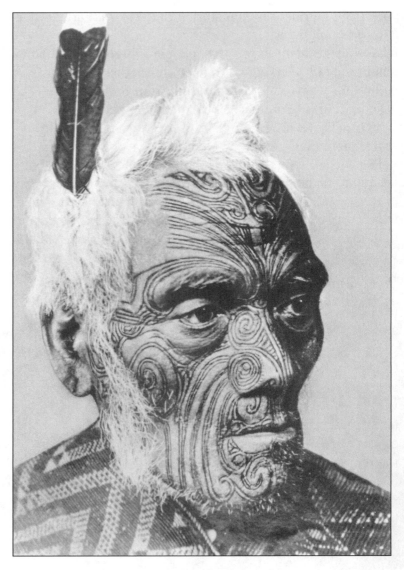

other regions, such as Africa and Central America, piercing became more popular. To decorate their bodies, tribes such as the Dogon of Mali and the Nuba of Ethiopia practiced lip piercing. The ancient Aztec and Maya of Central America pierced their tongues.

To England and the United States

It was not until the eighteenth century that tattooing was introduced to England and the United States. The British explorer Captain James Cook encountered tattooing in Tahiti and New Zealand between 1768 and 1771. Cook brought a tattooed Tahitian, Omai, to England. After seeing Omai's tattoos, English aristocrats became interested in getting tattoos of their own. Even royalty embraced tattooing. After visiting Jerusalem, the prince of Wales had the Jerusalem Cross, a religious symbol of four small crosses and one large cross, tattooed on his arm in 1862.

During the same period, body piercing also became popular among British aristocrats. Men wore the Prince Albert piercing, in which a ring was attached to a man's penis and then strapped to his thigh, to maintain the smooth line of tight trousers that were then in fashion. High-society British women embraced body piercing as well. In the late 1890s women wore low-cut dresses that revealed their nipples. The "bosom ring," a nipple piercing, became a fashionable way to decorate their nipples. Ear piercing also became popular among British women.

Both tattooing and piercing soon crossed the Atlantic Ocean to the United States. American women often read about and then embraced the fashion trends of British women. For this reason, by the end of the nineteenth century ear piercing became a common practice among American women. Tattooing made its way to the United States via the American navy. By the nineteenth century, 90 percent of all U.S. Navy sailors had tattoos. Initially, as in England, tattooing was popular not only with sailors but with the upper classes. However, this began to change in the later nineteenth century.

Rebel Practice

In 1891 American inventor Samuel O'Reilly devised the tattoo machine, which replaced the method of manually pricking the skin with inked needles. The tattoo machine has an electric motor that pushes a hollow needle filled with permanent ink in and out of the skin. This invention made it quicker and cheaper to get tattoos, and members of both the American and British working classes soon began to get them. Since tattoos could now easily be obtained by anyone, the practice was no longer as popular among aristocrats.

By the mid–twentieth century, tattooing had become a form of rebellion rather than a fashion statement. Margo DeMello, author of *Bodies of Inscription,* notes, "Bikers, gang members and convicts, while still a minority, were the public face of tattooing during this period alongside a lingering association with sailors."[2] Tattooing became considered by most a deviant practice. All piercing except ear piercing fell out of fashion with the upper and middle classes as well, and was considered as rebellious as tattooing.

Crossover to Mainstream

Tattoos and body piercing continued to be considered deviant activities in the United States until the 1960s, when

A woman in London gets a Union Jack tattooed on her shoulder in 1936. The invention of the tattoo machine in 1891 made tattooing popular among British and American working classes.

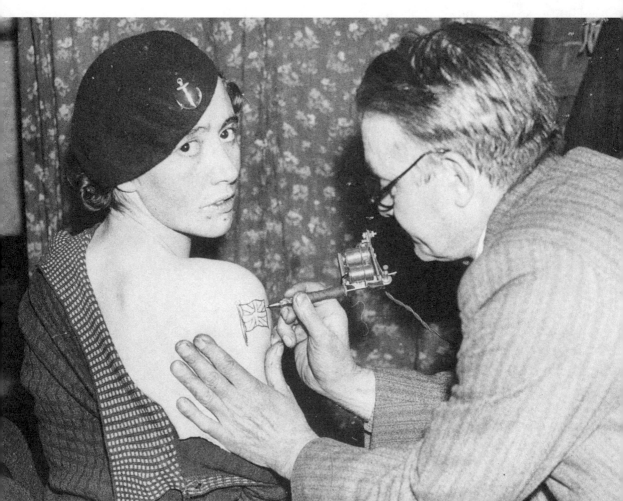

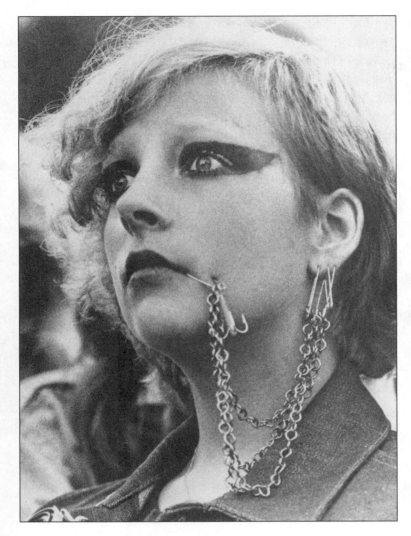

An English woman at the height of the punk craze in the 1970s displays multiple piercings on her face and ears.

both tattoos and body piercing began to cross over from the working class, bikers, prisoners, and military personnel to a younger, hipper audience. This crossover began with the hippies.

The hippies were a youth subculture who advocated universal love and peace and were associated with long hair, drugs, rock music, and political protests. The hippie culture embraced tattoos as a way to show the world their beliefs. They chose to get spiritual and political tattoos, such as yin-and-yang and peace signs. In addition, British youths who visited India during the 1960s adopted the Indian practice of piercing their noses. Piercing was adopted by the punk movement in the 1970s as a symbol of rebellion.

Tattoos and body piercing began to spread from rebellious youths to more mainstream society in the 1970s. This was due, in part, to the increasing professionalization of both industries. For example, Lyle Tuttle, a famous tattooist in San Francisco, realized that to attract new types of customers, tattooing had to lose its reputation for unhygienic practices. Tuttle was instrumental in getting new health regulations passed for tattoo studios. Because these regulations made getting a tattoo safer, more middle-class clients became interested in tattoos.

Body piercing also became more accessible to the public in the 1970s. Jim Ward opened the Gauntlet, the first U.S. body piercing studio. People could now get pierced by a professional rather than doing it themselves or having friends do it. And in 1989 the publication of *Modern Primitives,* a book featuring interviews with several people who had gotten piercings and tattoos, brought awareness of body piercing to readers throughout the United States.

In the years that followed, body piercing and tattooing continued to gain popularity among new groups of people. Many well-known artists, actors, musicians, and fashion designers adopted tattooing and piercing. The public followed this celebrity trend. By the end of the twentieth century both practices had become wildly popular.

1

Tattoos and Body Piercing Today

On February 2, 2004, an estimated 140 million people watched singers Janet Jackson and Justin Timberlake perform at the Super Bowl halftime show. At the end of the show, Timberlake ripped off part of Jackson's corset, exposing her breast, which was decorated with a nipple piercing. The incident shocked viewers and led to criticism of the network, Jackson, and Timberlake. However, the incident did benefit one segment of people—professional body piercers. Trilogy Body Piercings of Memphis, Tennessee, for example, has experienced a rise in sales of more than 40 percent since the 2004 Super Bowl Sunday, according to its owner, Lee Siegfried. Chris Fitzgerald, a professional piercer at Memphis Underground, reports a similar increase in business: "For so long, nipple piercings have been considered taboo—sexy but naughty. Janet is a pop icon, and she showed the world how good it can look. That's where the demand is coming from."[3]

The interest in nipple piercing is just one example of a celebrity inciting interest in permanent body art. Since the 1960s, when rock star Janis Joplin got a tattoo, celebrities have increasingly decorated their bodies with tattoos and body piercings. As a result, the mainstream public has followed their example and adopted the body art trend.

Famous Fad

Celebrities of all ages have tattooed and pierced their bodies. On the younger end of the spectrum, by age sixteen, singer Bow Wow had tattoos on his arm of his initials and a clown. By her early twenties, singer Britney Spears had several tattoos, including a fairy on her lower back and a small daisy circling the second toe on her right foot. Spears also has a pierced belly button and right nipple. On the other end of the age spectrum, at age fifty-four actor Harrison Ford had his ear pierced.

Entertainers are not the only public figures who have adopted body piercing and tattooing. Both practices have become widespread among public sports figures as well. In 1997 the Associated Press conducted a preseason survey of all twenty-nine NBA teams and reported that 35.1 percent of all professional basketball players had tattoos. In addition to his tattoos, former basketball player Dennis Rodman is well known for his nose ring and other body piercings. Piercing is not limited to basketball stars, however. Ricky Williams, college football's 1998 Heisman Trophy winner, wears a tongue stud. And in 2003 Brian Fell, a four-hundred-meter runner and hurdler at UCLA, started wearing a tongue ring and then a lower lip ring.

Other celebrities embracing body art include fashion designers and models. Designers Jean Paul Gaultier and Christian Lacroix introduced piercing on the Paris runways in 1994. That same year Suzy Menkes of the *New York Times* reported on the piercings of fashion models Christy Turlington and Naomi Campbell. "It is easy to pinpoint the moment when body piercing went mainstream," Menkes wrote.

> Christy Turlington came out at a London Fashion show, and in the middle of her navel was a ring! The next day Naomi Campbell showed the world that anything Christy could do, so could she. A gold ring with a small pear pierced her navel. And then at Isaac Mizrahi's show the two came out together, navels bared and beringed: body piercing as a Supermodel totem.[4]

Advertisements

As body piercing and tattoos became more mainstream, they began to appear in advertisements. For example, tattoos are seen in Marlboro and Silk Cut cigarette ads. Sony and Coca-Cola use tattoos in their print and television advertising. A large financial institution ran billboards that showed an arm with a tattoo of Federal Reserve chairman Alan Greenspan.

Tattoos have become so prevalent in ads that tattoo artists are commissioned by well-known companies to work on their advertising campaigns. New Jersey tattooist Shotsie Gorman received a commission from Absolut vodka to paint a full-body tattoo on a man yet leave a large blank space in

Former basketball superstar Dennis Rodman shows off his body piercings and his multiple tattoos. Among celebrities, body art is extremely fashionable.

the middle of his back in the shape of the Absolut Restraint bottle. The painted man's body was photographed and used as a print ad for Absolut Restraint.

Joe Tamargo has taken advertising and tattoos a step further. In 2005 Tamargo started selling advertisers the opportunity to tattoo their ads on his body. His first two customers were a California pharmaceutical company and SaveMartha.com, a

The original Barbie doll from the 1950s is shown opposite the Butterfly Art Tattoo Barbie introduced in 1999.

fan group of Martha Stewart. Each paid Tamargo to tattoo messages supporting their groups on his arm. By March 2005 he had nine sponsored tattoos, which earned him a total of $13,110.

Body Art Products

While some companies have used body art in advertising, others have manufactured products specifically related to tattoos and body piercings. These items are often intended for children. For example, in 1999 Mattel produced the Butterfly Art Tattoo Barbie and the Generation Girls. The Butterfly Art Tattoo Barbie doll's stomach was decorated with a tattoo. One of the Generation Girls, a friend of Barbie's, had a nose ring. Many parents argued that these products led to increased interest in tattoos and piercings among children. As a result of parental concern that these dolls could be a bad influence, in June 1999 Mattel Corporation stopped production of the Butterfly Art line.

Despite parental concern, the popularity of toys associated with tattoos and body piercings has grown. Temporary tattoos are bought and worn by children all over the world. Children can purchase items such as Crystal Tattoos and Jewelry by Natural Science Industry Limited, which includes temporary tattoos made of peel-and-stick rhinestones that firmly adhere to the skin. Although the Butterfly Art Tattoo Barbie is no longer available, parents can still buy their children dolls that are pierced or tattooed. Mattel recently produced the Cali Girl ear piercing doll, a Barbie doll that comes with a pretend ear piercer to pierce the doll's ears.

Popular Trend

Children are not the only ones interested in tattoos and body piercing. People of all ages and from all backgrounds are taking part in the body art trend. According to Kelly Luker, feature writer for the Silicon Valley paper *Metro,* "Judges, counselors, accountants, athletes and soccer moms are lining up outside the parlor doors for their own permanent body décor. And almost half of them return for more."[5]

Statistics back up Luker's assertion. A 2003 online survey by Harris Interactive found that 16 percent of all U.S.

adults have at least one tattoo. Health Canada reported that between 73 and 83 percent of U.S. women have their ears pierced. In addition, according to a 2002 study of 454 university students, more than half said they had a body piercing and about a quarter said they had a tattoo.

Although many people believe that body art is a trend of youth, statistics show that the person most likely to get tattooed and pierced is an adult of the postcollege age. Harris Interactive found that the age group with the highest number of tattoos is twenty-five- to twenty-nine-year-olds with 36 percent sporting tattoos, followed by thirty- to thirty-nine-year-olds with 28 percent.

Soccer Moms to Teenagers

Many of the adults drawn to tattooing are middle-class women. In fact, studies by medical journals, universities, and the media have found that the fastest growing segment of tattooists' clientele is middle-class, postcollege-age women. In 1997 Beth Seaton, professor of mass communications at York University, conducted a study of customers at one of Toronto, Canada's most popular tattoo art studios and found that 80 percent of them were upper-middle-class suburban females. And the 2003 Harris Interactive survey found that nearly the same percentage of American women as men have tattoos.

Kelly Luker also found that adult women are increasingly getting body art. "My 39-year-old friend Kimberly had her kids' names on her ankle, an elephant over her heart and the date of her sobriety permanently printed on the base of her spine," she wrote. "A 40-something co-worker has a rose on her upper arm and a heart over her heart."[6]

Adult women are not the only group of people who have been drawn to tattooing and piercing. According to a report edited by Dr. Lynn White of the Washington University School of Medicine, approximately 10 percent of twelve- to eighteen-year-olds are tattooed. A University of Rochester study showed that 4.4 percent of teenagers have some part of their body, other than their ears, pierced.

Body Art Controversies

As body art has become more popular among different seg-
ments of the population, a variety of issues and conflicts
have resulted. Many of these controversies are specifically
associated with teenage use of body art. Such controversies
range from yearbook displays to dress code policies.

In 2004, for example, the yearbook for Crothersville
Junior-Senior High School in Crothersville, Indiana, featured
a two-page, full-color spread titled "Body Decorations." The
spread contained photos of both students' and teachers'
tattoos and navel and tongue piercings. Many parents

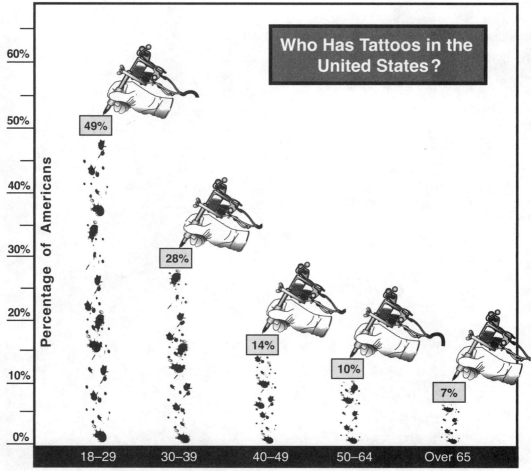

Who Has Tattoos in the United States?

Percentage of Americans

- 49%
- 28%
- 14%
- 10%
- 7%

18–29 30–39 40–49 50–64 Over 65

Ages of Americans With at Least One Tattoo

and school officials were upset by the photos. They believed that displaying the tattoos and body piercings was in poor taste and a disruption to the classroom; for those reasons, they felt the pictures should not be featured in the yearbook.

School officials were quick to react. Ralph Hillenburg, a Crothersville school trustee who received calls from people upset about the photos, stated that the photos should not have been allowed in the yearbook because such images violated the school dress code. Although the dress code did not ban facial piercings or tattoos, it did ban students from showing their navels at school.

A teenage girl shows off her tongue, eyebrow, and ear piercings. Many schools employ dress codes that forbid such body art.

Tom Judd, the principal of Crothersville Junior-Senior High School, said that he would review all yearbook pages in the future and that a yearbook spread like "Body Decorations" would not happen again. Other schools throughout the United States have dealt with similar controversies.

Dress Codes

One such issue is whether students should be allowed to have tattoos and body piercings at all. Another is what to do if a dress code forbidding body art is violated. These questions arose in 2004 in Henry County, Georgia.

On September 21 of that year, his second day at Dutchtown High School, fifteen-year-old Corey Rager was placed on in-school suspension for wearing eyebrow, nose, chin, and tongue piercings to school. The school's policy is that body piercing on any visible part of the body other than the ear, including the tongue, is prohibited. School officials believe the piercings disrupt school and are unsafe to its students.

A first offense of the dress code policy can lead to a one-day in-school suspension, in which a student comes to school but is placed in an isolated setting under supervision and is not allowed to attend his or her regular classes. A second offense results in a three-day suspension, but students can return to class if they remove the piercing. If they continue to violate the policy, they can receive an extended in-school suspension until they correct the violation. Because he refused to take out his piercings, Rager served in-school suspension for over a month, until his mother, Kati Monahan, decided to teach him at home.

Parents like Monahan believe that the decision to allow their children to wear piercings and tattoos should be up to them, not school officials. Several schools agree with Monahan's viewpoint and allow their students to wear visible piercings and tattoos. For example, in Fayette County, Georgia, high school students are allowed to wear multiple piercings provided they do not disrupt the learning process.

Body Art Changes

The controversies surrounding permanent body art have affected where people place tattoos and piercings on their bodies. Many students and professionals who get body art adorn themselves in areas that can be covered up by clothing. This allows them the freedom to get a tattoo or piercing yet avoid any issues in school or at the workplace.

Rodney Robinson, an executive at an international consulting company, has a tattoo of an archangel on his upper arm. He believes that tattoos are no longer automatically considered a detriment to a person's career. "[Having a tattoo] is viewed differently now," Robinson stated. "It is more acceptable and not considered outside of the norm."[7] However, Robinson acknowledges that body art can have a negative impact in the workplace if it becomes a distraction to others. For this reason, he chose to place his tattoo on his upper arm, which is typically covered by his shirtsleeve.

Decades ago, the most popular locations for men's tattoos were the front or back of the forearm. Today, men like Robinson often choose the upper arm or chest for tattoo locations because these areas are easier to cover with clothing. Women often ask that tattoos be placed on their ankles, hips, or lower backs, locations that can be concealed with clothing or are not immediately visible to other people. For example, at age twenty, Debra Knickerbocker got her tattoo, a white-sided angelfish, on her hip. "I specifically got it in an area that would rarely (if ever) be seen," Knickerbocker said. "I can even wear bathing suits that don't show it. I wanted to have the ability to hide it from my grandkids. I also didn't want my tattoo showing at my wedding."[8]

Many people who decide to get pierced in places other than the ear also take into consideration potential controversies. As with tattoos, people often choose to get pierced in areas that can be covered up with clothing. According to a survey reported in the November 2001 issue of *Clinical Nursing Research,* after the ear, the most popular body piercing locations are the tongue, nipple, and navel, all of which can either be covered up or are not immediately visible to others.

Tattoo Designs

The rising popularity of body art among students and professionals has led not only to changes in where people com-

Tattooed women commonly have their body art placed where it can easily be covered with clothing, such as the lower back.

monly choose to place their tattoos but to changes in the type of typical tattoo designs people choose. In the mid–twentieth century, neither tattoo clients nor tattoo artists were concerned with tattooing an artistic or aesthetically pleasing piece. The types of tattoos requested were either "Americana" types, ranging from eagles to anchors, or "vow" tattoos—tattoos of a person's name, typically a girlfriend's name or "Mom." The designs were made using thick black outlines filled in with solid blocks of color and had little detail. The tattoos were normally chosen from flash, sets of pictures drawn by artists that are reproduced and distributed to tattoo studios.

A typical client today wants a more detailed and artistic tattoo than those of the past. According to Clinton Sanders, author of *Customizing the Body: The Art and Culture of Tattooing,* "Coming from a higher socioeconomic background than the traditional tattooee, the new client commonly has more disposable income, emphasizes the decorative/aesthetic function of the tattoo over its affiliative/self-definitional function, and shares the tattoo artist's interest in the production of a uniquely creative and innovative custom-designed image."[9] In particular, custom designs of Japanese, tribal, and Chicano tattoos, all of which require detailed work, have become popular.

Japanese tattoos are large, often full-body, tattoos using bright colors. These tattoos are typically of heroic images from Japanese myths, such as samurai, dragons, and the phoenix. Tribal tattoos originated in areas such as Samoa and Hawaii. Their characteristics include heavy black lines and shading of geometric designs. Chicano tattoos are fine

A Japanese tattoo artist inks a full-body tattoo by hand. Unlike tattoos of the past, today's tattoo is often intricately detailed.

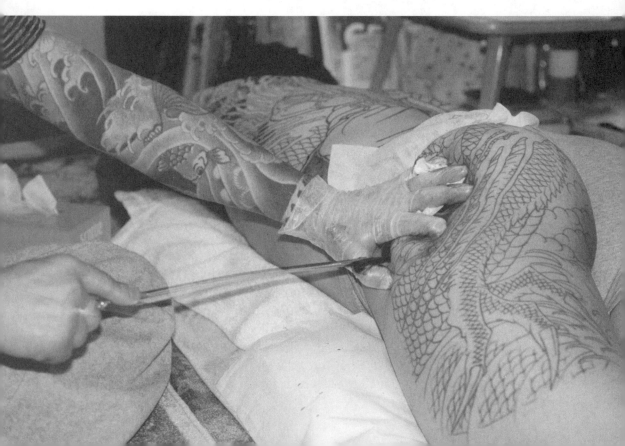

lined, have little color, and are highly detailed. They include photo-realistic portraits of people.

Tattooing as an Art?

The interest in custom work has led to changes in the kinds of people who become tattoo artists. In the early to mid–twentieth century, tattooists were more interested in the craft aspect of tattooing, focusing on the technical details such as building the tattoo machine and mixing the inks rather than the artistic aspect. They often learned the technical skills of tattooing from other tattooists. According to Sanders, "The traditional clientele consisted of young men from working-class backgrounds. . . . Practitioners were generally from the same social background as their clients, unassociated with the larger art world and primarily motivated by economic gain."[10]

Today, tattooists are often from artistic backgrounds and have chosen the field of tattooing as a way to practice art. Carl Williams, who has a master's degree in art from the University of Hawaii, is an example of a typical modern tattoo artist. "My original intention was to teach college art, but I started hanging out at nights at tattoo shops," Williams said. "After you've worked in different mediums, you can tell a big difference. I can get the skin to do more than paper."[11]

Pat Fish is another example of a tattooist with an artistic background. She earned degrees in studio art and film studies from the University of California Santa Barbara and taught drawing there after graduating. Fish opened a tattoo studio in Santa Barbara in 1984 so she could practice art full-time. She is best known for her Celtic designs, which are defined by intricate knotwork, braids, spirals, and circles. Clients come from all over the country for a Pat Fish original work.

The art community is beginning to consider tattoos a legitimate art form. Galleries and museums, such as the University of Pennsylvania Museum of Archaeology and Anthropology, are displaying photos of tattoos and body piercings along with living examples of body art. Art journals have also taken notice of body art. For example, the

July 1997 issue of *Art in America* featured an article on the work of artist Tony Fitzpatrick, founder of the World Tattoo Gallery in Chicago. Fitzpatrick's etchings and drawings are based, in part, on tattoo art.

Fad or Forever?

Whether or not body piercing and tattooing will continue to be considered an art form and increase in popularity are subjects of debate. Some believe that permanent body art is just a passing phase and that people will lose interest in getting pierced and tattooed. "I'm not under any illusions about fashion changes—I know body piercing is hip at the moment but times change so I don't expect to always have enough work,"[12] states Dave Bingham, a professional body piercer and tattoo artist who runs the largest and best-known salon in Ireland.

However, statistics show that permanent body art may not be just a passing fad. Instead, like cosmetics, it could become a long-term fashion mainstay. In recent years, the number of people getting tattooed or pierced has increased annually. A May 1996 issue of the medical journal *Physician's Assistant* estimated that in the preceding twenty years, tattooing among women quadrupled. The number of tattoo studios throughout the United States has also increased. In 1994 there were 137 tattoo studios registered in Texas, for example. Eight years later that number had increased to over 600. In addition, the Alliance of Professional Tattooists (APT), a national organization of registered tattooists, reported that its membership grew from 1,800 members in 1999 to 3,000 members in 2004.

The body piercing industry is also experiencing growth. According to International Collection, a New York City body-jewelry wholesaler, the wholesale body-jewelry industry was an estimated $3 billion business in 2003 and is projected to double or triple in the next few years. States have also reported evidence of piercing's popularity. According to the *Portland Mercury,* in 2001 there were 695 licensed body piercing technicians in Oregon, an increase of 250 percent since 1996.

Many people believe that tattooing and body piercing have continued to grow in popularity because an increasing number of people are getting tattooed and pierced for personal reasons rather than because they are following a fashion trend. Whether or not body piercing and tattooing will continue to gain popularity depends on how strong these personal reasons are.

A woman winces in pain while getting tattooed. Statistics suggest that permanent body art may be more than just the latest fad.

2

Why Do People
Get Body Art?

PEOPLE WHO CHOOSE to get pierced choose to experience pain. A person who gets a piercing must endure a hollow needle being forced through his or her skin or cartilage without use of an anesthetic. Tattooing also involves pain. When being tattooed, a person receives an injection of pigment particles under the skin at a rate of fifty to three thousand times per minute with an electric tattoo machine. Depending on the tattoo's size, a person may have to endure the needles poking his or her skin from thirty minutes to several sessions of an hour or more. Despite the pain, for thousands of years millions of people have willingly subjected themselves to tattooing and piercing. Their reasons for getting permanent body art overcome any fear they might have of the pain.

Ancient people's reasons for getting tattoos or body piercings varied depending on where they lived. For example, the ancient Aztec and Maya of Central America practiced tongue piercing as a way to create an altered state of consciousness so that they could communicate with the gods. The New Zealand Maori tattooed themselves both to commemorate rites of passage and as a way to display their tribal status. Japanese men would tattoo themselves with intricate Irezumi designs, designs that displayed heroic figures, gods, and mythical creatures, as a way to decorate their bodies.

Today people get pierced or tattooed for many of the same reasons ancient people did. Their reasons range from getting tattooed to commemorate a particular accomplishment, such as graduating from college, to getting their nose pierced to be fashionable. Ultimately, people endure the pain of permanent body art so that they can outwardly display parts of their inner selves. "A tattoo is never just what the appearance is, anyway. You can only really know about the tattoo by getting to know the person wearing it. Tattoos are indicators, or little vents to their psyche,"[13] states Don Ed Hardy, a well-known tattooist and former editor of *Tattootime*.

Enhancing Beauty

Often people get tattooed or pierced because they believe it enhances their beauty. For example, some people choose

A woman endures the pain of a tongue piercing. Body art is most commonly perceived as an outward expression of the inner self.

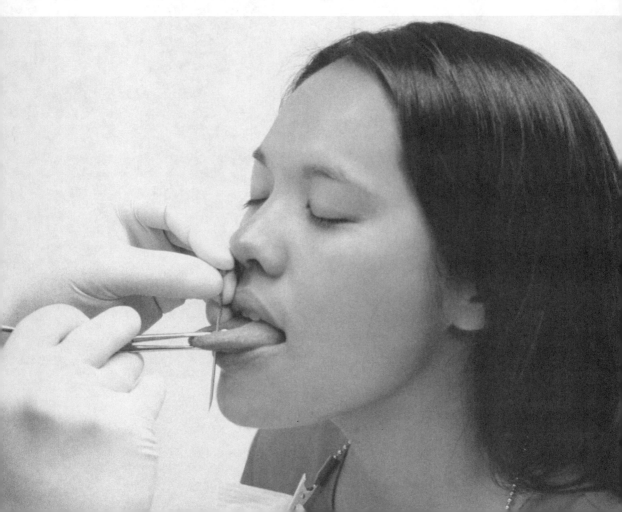

tattoos that follow the contours of a certain body part to make it look thinner and shapelier. Others choose body art to emphasize a part of their body that they like. Women pleased with the shape of their stomachs often choose navel piercings.

Others use tattoos as a way to cover up their scars or birthmarks. Jean-Chris Miller, author of *The Body Art Book,* writes about a woman who got tattooed after she had a hysterectomy. The procedure left the woman with a scar across her abdomen. Even though she did not consider herself the type of person who typically gets tattoos, she had a line of flowers inked over the scar to camouflage it. She has been

Many people resort to body art as a beauty enhancement. This woman enhances the contours of her stomach with jewelry in her navel.

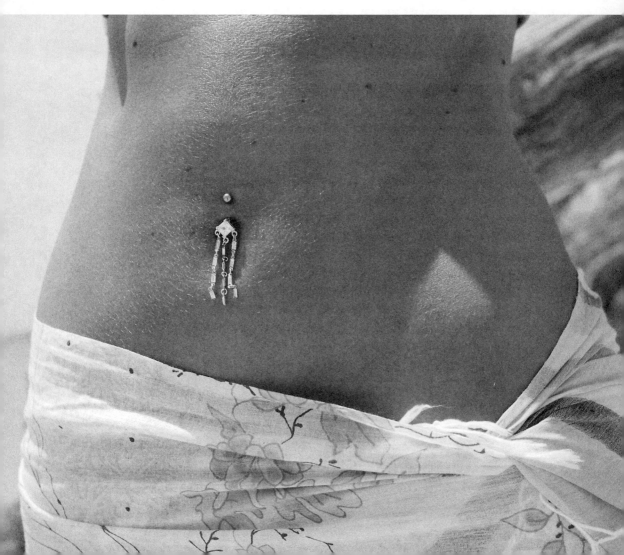

happy with the results and is considering getting more tattoos.

Some women also choose to have micropigmentation, the tattooing of permanent makeup onto the face, as a way to enhance their beauty. The process of getting micropigmentation is the same as getting a decorative tattoo, except that the ink does not go in as deep. Micropigmentation tattoos replicate eyebrows, eyeliner, lipstick, and other facial enhancements. Some women decide to get these tattoos so they no longer have to apply cosmetics to their faces.

Another segment of women who get micropigmentation are those who have undergone chemotherapy and have lost their hair, including their eyebrows. Using micropigmentation to create eyebrows helps these women feel more confident of their appearance.

Besides enhancing beauty, another reason people choose to get piercings and tattoos is to feel better both physically and psychologically. For example, many people who have genital or nipple piercings claim to have enhanced sexual experiences. Others say their body art makes them feel more attractive and self-confident. According to a recent Harris Poll, almost half of all tattooed women said that they feel sexier with their body art.

Another commonly cited reason for getting permanent body art is simply for decoration. "Tattooing is really just a form of personal adornment," explains a tattoo artist in *Customizing the Body*. "Why does someone get a new car and get all of the paint stripped off it and paint it candy-apple red? Why spend $10,000 on a car and then spend another $20,000 to make it look different from the car you bought? I associate it with ownership. Your body is one of the things you indisputably own. There is a tendency to adorn things that you own to make them especially yours."[14] Backing this assertion, a 2001 study published in *Clinical Nursing Research* reports that, of those surveyed, 62 percent who pierced their bodies and 40 percent who tattooed their bodies did so to express their individuality.

Identifying Oneself

Another important reason that people get pierced or tattooed is to commemorate an event or rite of passage that

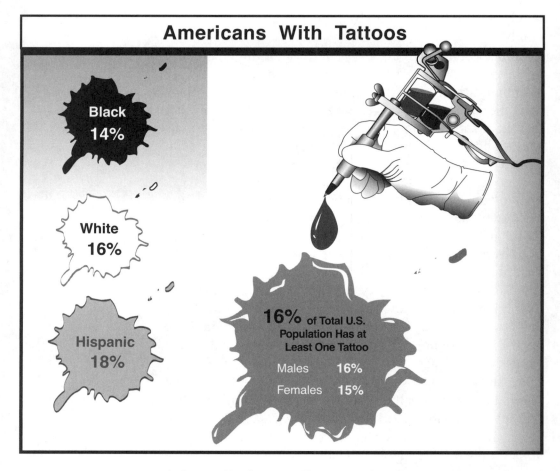

Americans With Tattoos

Black
14%

White
16%

Hispanic
18%

16% of Total U.S.
Population Has at
Least One Tattoo

Males   16%
Females   15%

defines who they are. For example, some people get pierced or tattooed to celebrate a milestone such as turning twenty-one years old. Others want to commemorate a new phase of life after a traumatic event such as a divorce. A woman interviewed for the book *Customizing the Body* got her first tattoo when her marriage failed. "I finally really decided [to get a tattoo] sometime last year when my marriage was coming apart," she explained. "It started as a symbol of taking my body back. I was thinking that about the time I got divorced would be a good time to do it."[15]

Besides memorializing significant events, people can use tattoos to outwardly express beliefs important to them. For example, religious symbols are used to show a person's spiritual beliefs. Christian body art is especially popular, and includes tattoos such as praying hands, the Virgin

Mary, or the crucifixion of Christ. In fact, the Christian Tattoo Association formed specifically for tattooed Christians and Christian tattoo artists. The group's members combine their faith with their love for the art of tattooing.

Tattoos are also used to show people's allegiance to certain groups. As an example, military personnel often pick tattoos that relate to their service. A navy sailor may choose an anchor for his tattoo. Other members of groups, such as sports teams, may visit tattoo shops together and all get the same tattoo to show their devotion to their team.

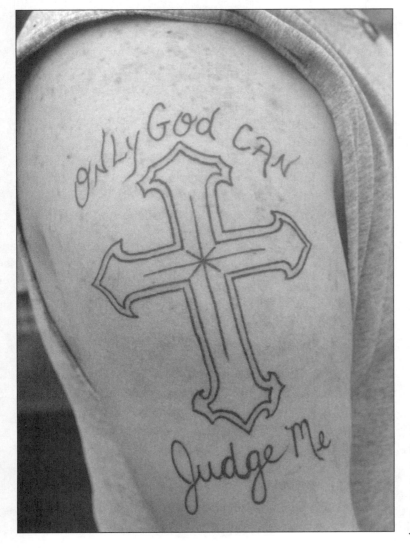

Tattoos are often reflections of religious or spiritual beliefs. Here, a man expresses his conviction that only his maker can judge him.

Similarly, gang members use tattoos as a way to display what gang they belong to. For instance, if a gang member sports a tattoo of a black hand with a letter "M" on the palm, it indicates that he is affiliated with the Mexican Mafia. Even though tattoos can help police identify and track gang members, gang members still get them because the tattoos are a way to tell the world who they are.

Commemorating Others

Many people get body art to show their love and commitment to someone who is important to them. By the mid–twentieth century, vow tattoos, tattoos of the names of people, were among the most popular types of tattoos. According to author Margo DeMello, the most popular vow tattoos included the names "Mom," "Mother," and a sweetheart's name.

Today vow tattoos continue to be popular, and many celebrities have them. Famous soccer player David Beckham, for example, has his wife's name, Victoria; his son's name, Brooklyn; and his other son's name, Romeo, tattooed on various parts of his body. His wife, famous for being Posh Spice in the pop group the Spice Girls, in turn has Beckham's initials tattooed on her body.

In addition to vow tattoos, people get symbols tattooed on their bodies to show their attachment to a loved one. "This tattoo is a symbol of friendship," said a person interviewed for the book *Customizing the Body*. "Me and my best friend—I've known him since I could walk—came in together and we both got bluebirds to have a symbol that when we do part we will remember each other by it."[16]

Portrait tattoos, tattoos of people's faces using fine lines and details, are another popular way of commemorating a person. People getting portrait tattoos often have a portrait of a child, spouse, or someone who has influenced their lives tattooed onto their bodies. For example, singer Fred Durst of Limp Bizkit has portrait tattoos of rock stars Elvis Presley and Kurt Cobain on his chest.

Taking Control

Another reason people get body piercings and tattoos is that they believe their body art acts as a talisman, giving them

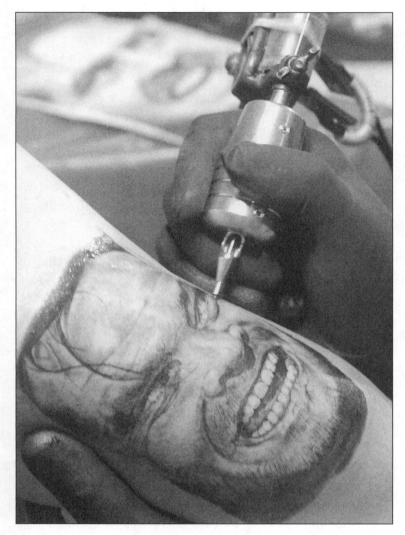

This man pays homage to his favorite actor, Jack Nicholson, with a tattoo of a still shot from the movie The Shining.

strength and protection or the courage to change their lives. This type of body art can range from something simple, such as a tattoo of a lucky number, to the complex, such as a tattoo of an entire prayer. "My first tattoo is a dragon on my back. I got it because it's both my Chinese astrological symbol and I considered it as well my 'totem,'" explains a woman interviewed for the book *Bodies of Inscription.* "I felt that it gave me strength. I was going through a difficult time in my relationship and was unhappy with the direction my life was taking. So I quit school, got a job as a cocktail waitress, got this tattoo and got my nose pierced—all in the same week. I felt these decisions were instrumental in helping me turn my life around."[17]

Studies show that adolescents, as well as adults, often turn to tattoos and body piercing as a way to gain control of their lives. In a 1997 article for the *Journal of the American Academy of Child and Adolescent Psychiatry,* Andres Martin wrote that tattoos give some adolescents a sense of normalcy and control over their changing bodies. He also found that when dealing with major changes in their lives, such as divorce, foster care placement, and repeated moves, adolescents felt that tattoos provided them with stability. Because tattoos are unchanging and permanent, they gave the adolescents a sense of constancy.

Whereas adolescents get tattooed to deal with the changes in their lives, women who have been raped or sexually abused sometimes get tattooed or pierced to symbolically regain control of their bodies. "In some of these cases, experiencing the pain of metal struck through private parts serves as a liberation of the formerly felt emotional pain,"[18] says Aglaja Stirn, assistant director of the Frankfurt University Teaching Hospital for Psychosomatic Medicine and Psychotherapy in Germany. She believes that for some women, piercing is a way of reclaiming body parts from memories of abuse.

Modern Primitives

Like the women who get body art as a way to reclaim their bodies, people who get pierced and tattooed as part of the "modern primitive" movement, a movement in which people perform ancient rituals such as piercing and tattooing, embrace the pain of permanent body art. The movement gained many followers after the 1989 publication of *Modern Primitives,* a book that includes interviews with several famous body modifiers, including Fakir Musafar. Musafar, who coined the term *modern primitive* in 1967, believes that a modern primitive is a person who responds to primal urges by getting body modifications such as piercing and tattooing. Modern primitives feel that modern society lacks rituals that bind people together. By undergoing the pain and ritual of getting pierced or tattooed, Musafar believes people are able to reconnect with their identity and to society.

As a result of this movement, tattooists and body piercers are incorporating rituals, upon request, when tattooing or piercing their clients. According to DeMello, one East Coast tattooist offers "ceremonial tattooing," which includes the offering of food, flowers, and gifts to an altar at the tattoo studio. Other rituals performed by body piercers and tattooists include burning candles, consulting an astrology chart to choose an auspicious date for a person to get body art, and inviting loved ones to view the process.

Some body artists incorporate rituals when tattooing or piercing clients. Burning candles is one such ritual.

Rebellious Acts

Modern primitives use body art as a way to rebel against modern society; others get pierced or tattooed to rebel against people. Despite the increasing popularity of body art, many people continue to view piercing and tattooing as rebellious activities. In particular, parents of adolescents often view permanent body art as an act of defiance. For this very reason, some teenagers choose to get body art. Connor Kamada, an international business and French student at UCLA, has an eyebrow and ear cartilage pierced. "My parents hated it," said Kamada. "They didn't think that it was very normal, but that's the whole appeal of it—to rebel." [19]

Teenagers are not the only people who get body art as a defiant act. Although body art is becoming more popular each year, currently only 16 percent of American adults have tattoos and 2 percent report having one or more piercings other than ear. Those adults who get piercings and tattoos often do so as a way to enjoy the unconventional sides of themselves. Author Jean-Chris Miller writes of a woman who got piercings for just this reason: "If you saw her on the street, she would look like any corporate type, in conservative clothes and sensible shoes. But Kai has a secret. Under her navy-blue suit she sports many sexy piercings. She says she enjoys the metal in her body . . . because it's a way to express her wild side while protecting her professional image." [20]

Pushing Boundaries

Some people are not satisfied with getting a few piercings or tattoos. To achieve a sense of uniqueness, they have taken body art to new limits. For example, some choose to be different by getting full bodysuit tattoos, tattoos connected on the front and back of the torso and along the arms and legs.

Full-body tattoos date back to the 1600s, when they became popular in Japan. These tattoos encompassed connected designs of warriors, battle scenes, and mythical

creatures. Sailor Jerry Collins, a famous American tattooist, introduced the Japanese full bodysuit tattoo to U.S tattooing in the 1960s. Since then, it has become popular among those who want to push the boundaries of conventional tattooing.

Bill Salmon, a tattooist in San Francisco, believes that the biggest change in tattooing today is "the idea of a tattoo as a full body concept—not just a badge or sticker on the body. At the San Diego Tattoo Convention a few years ago Nakano [Horiyoshi III] got onstage and showed a full body suit done 25 years ago that looked immaculate; a real example of high standards and quality. So the new ideal is: having the vision comprehensive enough so that whatever specific tattoos you get are just part of a bigger plan."[21]

This student's body art may reflect an attitude of defiance. Tattoos and piercings are common symbols of rebellion.

Salmon himself has a full bodysuit of tattoos accumulated from forty-seven different tattooists.

While people like Salmon have chosen to decorate their entire bodies with tattoos, others have chosen to pierce as much of their bodies as possible. Elaine Davidson decided she wanted to have the most piercings of any woman in the world. She achieved this with 2,250 piercings. Another piercer also recently achieved a world record. Brian Moffatt, a thirty-four-year-old Canadian, set the record for the most number of piercings obtained in one setting. Moffatt, a professional piercer, pushed 702 needles into his body in less than eight hours. The majority of the piercings went into his legs and feet. He said his reason for pursuing the world record was that he wanted to be different from everybody else.

Body Makeovers

Some people have embraced piercing and tattooing as a way to transform themselves. Among the most famous of these body modifiers are Tom Leppard, also known as Leopard Man; Cat Man; and Enigma. Each of these men completely transformed his body with tattoos for different reasons.

Leppard, of Isle of Skye, Scotland, is a former soldier who has 99.9 percent of his body tattooed with a leopard-skin design. The only parts of his body that do not have tattoos are the insides of his ears and the skin between his toes. After serving in the military, Leppard chose to get tattooed and drop out of society. He lives in a hut made of sticks and stones, bathes in a river, and once a week goes by canoe to buy supplies. "I spent too long in the forces, 28 years. I couldn't mix with ordinary people," Leppard said, explaining his reason for transforming his body. "I decided I wanted to be the biggest of something, the only one of something. It had to be a tattoo, one tattoo. This is one tattoo."[22]

Dennis Smith, a computer programmer, also has tattoos resembling an animal. Smith, who legally changed his name to "Cat Man," is tattooed from head to toe with orange and

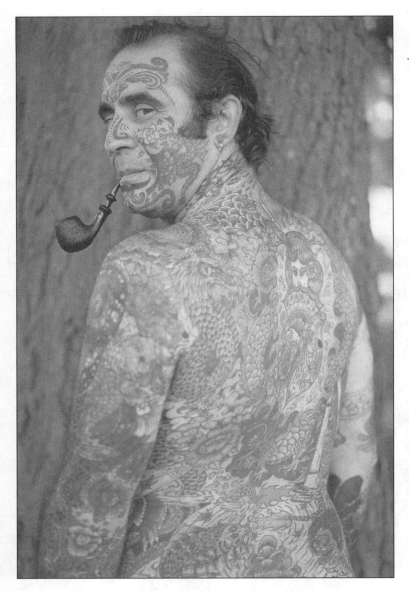

This man has used his entire body as a canvas for tattoos. Full-body tattooing is steadily growing in popularity.

black stripes. His teeth have also been filed to points, he has had latex whiskers implanted, and he underwent surgery to make his lips into a permanent snarl. Cat Man now wants a surgeon to graft tiger fur onto his skin. His ultimate goal is to transform himself as close to a tiger as possible because he believes that is who he is meant to be.

Enigma is also tattooed all over his body, including his face and head. His tattoos are mainly of blue puzzle pieces.

He has been tattooed by over 180 artists around the world, from South Africa to Switzerland. Unlike Leppard and Cat Man, Enigma did not get tattoos to separate himself from society or to become an animal. Instead, his tattoos are a part of his performance act. Enigma's career as a performer involves swallowing swords, lifting weights with his eyeballs, displaying his tattooed body, and singing.

New Modifications

The popularity of body piercing and tattooing has led to new body art trends. One of the new trends is scarification, the de-

Tattooed with blue puzzle pieces, the entertainer Enigma performs his sword-swallowing act in Seattle, Washington, in 1995.

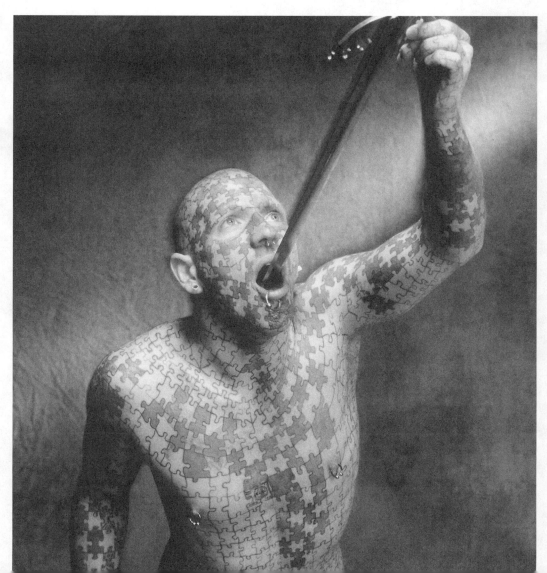

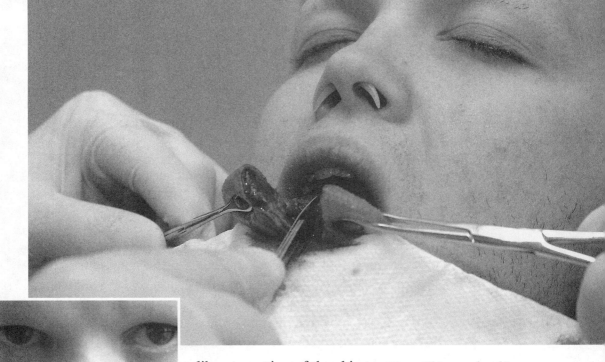

This man has his tongue split as a form of extreme body art. After the procedure, he shows off his cleanly forked tongue (inset).

liberate cutting of the skin to create scars. This practice dates back thousands of years. The indigenous people of New Zealand and Australia were the first to practice scarification. Today, people all over the world get scars by cutting themselves or by practitioners who use a surgical scalpel or laser. The designs range from the simple, with straight lines, to the more intricate, with spirals.

Another body art trend rising in popularity is branding. Branding is the burning of the skin, usually with hot metal, to leave a scar of a design. In ancient times, branding was a way to show ownership of a slave or livestock. Today, those who get branded often do so to show allegiance to a group. Branding is becoming common on college campuses among African American fraternities. For example, basketball star Michael Jordan has his fraternity brand on his chest.

An even more extreme form of body modification is tongue splitting. During this procedure, a person's tongue is cut down the middle, leaving a forked tongue. This process is typically done using a laser, heated blade, or scalpel. Historically, tongue splitting was a Hatha and Kumbhaka yoga practice, in which the tongue was first split and then used in breathing exercises. Shannon Larratt, editor and publisher of *Body Modification Ezine,* had his tongue split in 1997. He writes that modern tongue splitting began in 1997 and, by the year 2003, nearly two thousand people in the West had undergone the process. Larratt claims that people split their tongues mainly because they like the look of it and the sensation in their mouths.

Technology is also opening the doors to new ways to decorate the body. Dutch eye surgeons have recently implanted jewelry called "JewelEye" in the mucous membrane of the eyes of six women and one man. The Ophthalmic Surgery Research and Development Institute in Rotterdam pioneered this type of cosmetic surgery. The procedure involves inserting a 0.13-inch-wide (0.33cm) piece of specially developed jewelry, such as a half-moon or a heart, into the eye's mucous membrane under local anesthetic. Since the membrane is clear, people can see the implant clearly against the white of the eye. The Rotterdam institute claims that it has a waiting list for people who want the eye implant.

As people continue to seek unique ways to express who they are, they will push body art to new levels. According to Kelly Rothenberg, who writes for *Body Modification Ezine,* "What was once taboo is now becoming mainstream, and in fact has become so mainstream that body art has already moved on to the next level with body piercing, which will also continue to push the mainstream acceptance envelope until either something else comes along to surpass it, or society snaps backwards to ultra-conservancy once again."[23]

3

Health Issues

PHYSICIANS RECOMMEND THAT before getting a tattoo or piercing, people need to understand the potential health issues associated with body art. Getting pierced or tattooed can result in both minor and major health problems. By understanding what these risks are, people can take precautions to prevent or reduce them.

The most dangerous health risk associated with permanent body art is getting infected with a bloodborne disease, a disease that is passed by contamination of blood. This happens if the tattoo needle or piercing needle has been previously used on another person who has a disease. Pathogens, disease-causing organisms, can live in dried blood for several days and in liquid blood for even longer. An individual receiving a tattoo or piercing can come into contact with a pathogen if the equipment used has not been sterilized since its last use. Because of the risk, the American Red Cross requires that people wait a year after getting a tattoo to donate blood. The Red Cross also requires that people wait to donate blood for a year after they are pierced if they are unsure whether sterile needles were used during the piercing.

The most feared bloodborne disease is HIV. HIV is a mutating retrovirus that attacks the human immune system and has been shown to cause acquired immunodefiency syndrome (AIDS). AIDS results in the progressive destruction of a person's immune system, eventually leaving him or her unable to fight off colds and infections. Many AIDS symptoms are treatable, but the disease itself is incurable and always leads to death. To date, there have been no documented cases of tattooing or piercing resulting in HIV, but people fear this because the possibility exists.

Hepatitis

HIV and AIDS are not the only potential health risks associated with piercings and tattoos. "The primary fear most people express about getting tattooed or pierced is that they may contract the HIV virus, which may cause AIDS," writes Jean-Chris Miller, author of *The Body Art Book*. "HIV is only one of many viruses that can be transmitted. Syphilis, tuberculosis, strep, staph, and hepatitis are just a few of the other diseases to take into consideration."[24] In particular, hepatitis B and hepatitis C are among the most serious diseases that can result from shared needles.

Professional tattoo artists like this man take precautions against infection. Tattooing and piercing carry a serious risk of transmitting blood-borne diseases.

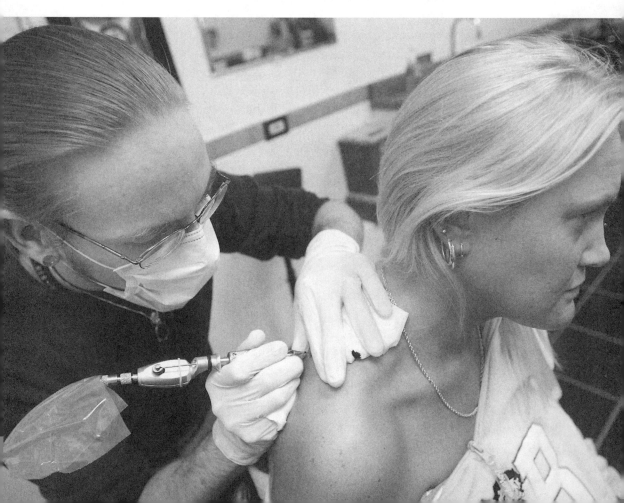

Hepatitis C is often associated with amateur tattooing. Prisoners with do-it-yourself tattoos like this man are at a very high risk of contracting the disease.

Hepatitis B can cause lifelong infection, cirrhosis (scarring) of the liver, liver cancer, liver failure, and death. Like those of AIDS, hepatitis B symptoms are treatable, but there is no known cure. According to the National Institute of Environmental Health Sciences, there have been cases of hepatitis B being transmitted through tattooing.

A recent study by a former Centers for Disease Control (CDC) researcher also suggests that getting a tattoo can significantly increase a person's chances of getting hepatitis C. Hepatitis C is an incurable disease that is transmitted through blood. It is a viral infection of the liver that often leads to fatal liver disease. "People who had do-it-yourself tattoos have a three times greater risk for hepatitis C than people without tattoos, and people tattooed in jail have an even higher risk. But the greatest risk comes from commercial tattoo parlors," states Robert Haley, chief of epidemiology at the University of Texas Southwestern Medical Center in Dallas. "People who get tattoos at commercial tattoo parlors have a nine times greater risk."[25] Haley's risk calculations are based on a study of over 600 people who were patients at a spine clinic in the early 1990s. His evaluation included information about lifestyle risk factors and blood tests. Haley found that out of 113 patients who had at least one tattoo, 22 percent tested positive for hepatitis C. Only 3.5 percent of the patients with no tattoos had hepatitis C.

Infections

Infections caused by pathogenic microorganisms invading the body are another health risk associated with tattoos and piercings. These infections can occur because the needles open the skin, allowing bacteria to enter the body, and can range from mild to life threatening.

Piercings have a greater tendency than tattoos to become infected. According to a Mayo Clinic article, studies show that up to 30 percent of piercings result in infections. This is because often the piercing needle goes through flesh, whereas tattoo needles only penetrate the skin. Piercings are also prone to infections because they have long healing times, ranging from six weeks for an earlobe to six months for a navel piercing; because they rub against clothing; and because unsterilized jewelry may harbor bacteria. Navel piercings are among the most common piercings to result in infections because tight-fitting clothing inhibits air circulation, allowing moisture to collect in the piercing.

The American Academy of Dermatology warns people to be careful when getting any form of body piercing, except ear piercing, because of possible skin infections. Typical symptoms include redness and swelling of the skin around the area that has been pierced and pus discharging from the piercing. Ointments are often used to cure minor infections.

More serious infections may require antibiotics or surgery and can result in long-lasting effects. For example, nipple piercing infections may affect a woman's ability to breastfeed. Infections in the upper ear can also be very serious. Upper-ear cartilage does not have its own blood supply, so

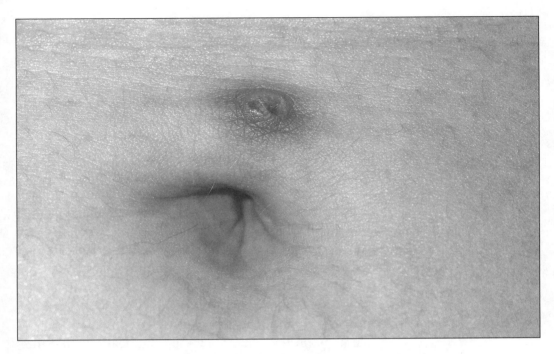

taking antibiotics is often ineffective because drugs cannot travel to the infection site. Upper-ear skin infections may require surgical drainage of pus. The most serious of these infections can permanently deform the ear.

This photo shows an infected piercing near a woman's navel. Without proper care of the wound, bacteria enter and infect the piercing site.

At Greater Risk

Among the most dangerous of piercing infections is endocarditis, a life-threatening infection of the heart valves. People with congenital heart disease who get pierced are particularly susceptible to getting endocarditis. Left untreated, the infection can fatally destroy the heart muscle. A Mayo Clinic study of 445 patients with congenital heart disease found that nearly one out of four of these patients developed endocarditis after getting pierced.

The January 2003 issue of the *Pediatric Infectious Disease Journal* stated that doctors are reporting increasing numbers of people developing infectious endocarditis after body piercing. The article included an example of a thirteen-year-old girl who became seriously ill one month after piercing her own navel. She was born with a heart malformation that had been surgically corrected when she was three years old. The girl said she had removed her piercing after two days because it looked infected. A month later, she went to the doctor after running a fever for three days. Tests revealed that she had an infection in one of her heart's valves. The girl was treated with heart surgery and antibiotics and released from the hospital after twenty-two days.

In addition to individuals with congenital heart disease, people with medical conditions such as diabetes and hemophilia are at a greater risk than most when getting pierced or tattooed. Diabetics take longer than nondiabetics to heal from cuts. The lengthier healing time increases their chances of getting an infection. While a diabetic's main risk is infection, the danger for a hemophiliac is that he or she will lose excessive amounts of blood when getting pierced or tattooed. Typically when a person is cut, the blood's ability to clot heals the wound, but a hemophiliac's blood does not clot properly. This can result in great blood loss.

Like hemophiliacs, people taking medications that thin the blood are at risk of their blood not clotting when cut. Blood-thinning medications can make a person more likely to bleed heavily during and after the tattoo or piercing process, and to experience excessive scabbing afterward.

Beyond Infections

Less dangerous but more common health problems associated with tattoos and body piercings are those that negatively affect one's appearance. One such problem is keloids, scars that grow beyond normal boundaries. People with darker pigmentation, such as African Americans and those of Mediterranean descent, have a greater risk of developing keloids. Keloids can develop after the initial tattooing or piercing or later, if the jewelry in a piercing catches on something and rips the skin. Often keloids can be removed only by surgery.

Another cosmetic complication is chipped teeth. This complication is specifically associated with oral piercings. Once the tongue is pierced, the jewelry may chip or crack a person's teeth when he or she is talking or eating. Tongue piercings can also result in more serious health problems.

For example, a person may develop a lisp or have trouble swallowing due to nerve damage in the tongue. The American Dental Association cites numerous other dangers associated with oral piercings, including the swelling of the tongue from the piercing; choking on studs, barbells, or hoops that come loose in the mouth; and uncontrollable bleeding.

Emergency Care

Another danger of tattoos and piercings is that they can adversely affect emergency care. For example, some doctors

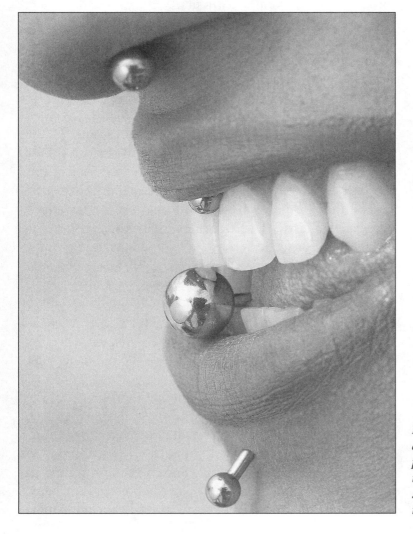

Piercing can negatively affect body function. A pierced tongue, for instance, can lead to severe nerve damage in the organ.

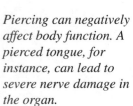

believe that passing a needle through the pigment of a tattoo may pose a significant health risk, leading to possible neurological complications later on in life. Theoretically, if a needle is passed through a lower-back tattoo, then a pigment-containing tissue core from the tattoo could be deposited into the spaces surrounding the spinal area. Doctors believe it is possible that this could cause long-term problems such as arachnoiditis, a chronic inflammatory process affecting the protective membranes around the brain, spinal cord, and nerve roots. Because of this potential, doctors try to avoid inserting a needle through a tattoo. This can create problems during emergency care, particularly for pregnant women with lower-back tattoos.

Pregnant women often require an epidural anesthesia when they go into labor. This type of anesthesia is injected through the lower back into the lumbar interspace, the space surrounding the membrane that covers the spinal cord. If a woman has a lower-back tattoo, finding a tattoo-free location for the epidural could be difficult or impossible.

According to the Food and Drug Administration (FDA), magnetic resonance imaging (MRI), a procedure that produces a two-dimensional view of an internal organ or structure, is another medical procedure that can be negatively affected by tattoos. An MRI is often used to diagnose sports-related injuries and chronic disease conditions. Some people have experienced burning or swelling in their tattooed areas when they have undergone an MRI. There have also been reports that tattoo pigments have interfered with the quality of the MRI. This has mainly occurred with people who had permanent eyeliner from micropigmentation. The theory is that the metallic components in some of the pigments interact with the MRI.

Like tattoos, body piercings can cause problems during emergency care. For example, oral piercings can result in tongue rips during certain procedures. "The potential for trouble arises in emergency situations when the patient needs to be intubated—that is, have a breathing tube inserted down his or her throat—to receive urgent care," states Sandra Tunajek, director of practice for the American Association of Nurse Anesthetists. "A pierced tongue isn't typically the first thing on the anesthesia provider's mind while they're preparing the patient for surgical or some other emergency care. The instrument used to insert the breathing tube may catch on the tongue ring, tearing the tongue or knocking the ring down the patient's throat."[26]

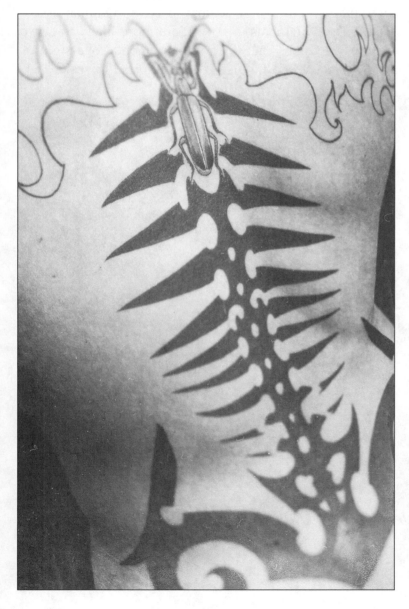

A tattoo on the lower back may cause complications with administering epidural anesthesia to pregnant women. For this reason, doctors avoid inserting needles through tattoos.

Allergic Reactions

Allergic reactions are also a potential danger of tattoos and piercings. Tattoo colors are made by mixing dry pigments with a suspension fluid. More than fifty different pigments and shades are used in tattooing. Tattoo pigments can be made from a variety of materials, ranging from vegetable matter to plastic-based pigments like acrylic. Organic-based tattoo pigments are seldom reactive to human tissue; plastic-based pigments, however, are more likely to cause allergic reactions. There is no governmental oversight of these substances. Although several color additives are ap-

Plastic-based pigment used in tattoo ink can trigger severe allergic reactions in some people.

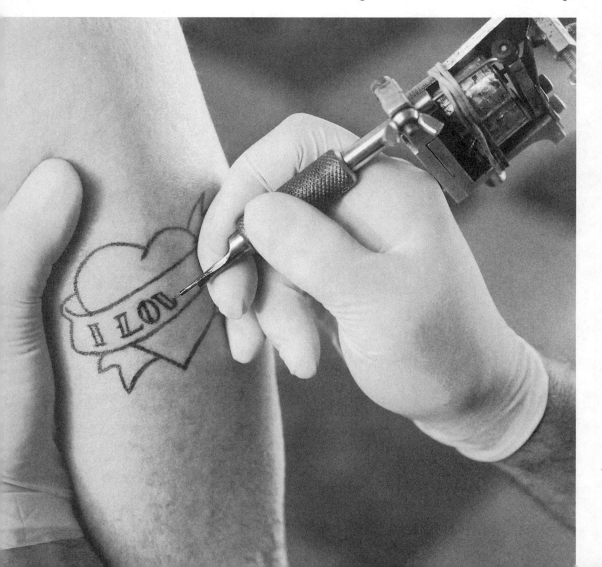

proved by the FDA for use in cosmetics, which are applied on the skin, the FDA does not regulate the use of color additives in the practice of tattooing, in which inks are injected into the skin.

Minor allergic reactions to the tattoo dyes typically result in an itchy rash at the tattoo site. More serious reactions include the development of granulomas, nodules that form around material the body perceives as foreign. Severe allergies can result in shortness of breath, rapid heartbeat, and fever.

Like tattoo dyes, piercing jewelry can cause allergic reactions. Brass-plated, nickel, and gold jewelry are the most likely types to cause allergic reactions. A piercing allergy often results in a weeping, itchy wound around the piercing. At times the body may react by pushing out the jewelry.

Risky Behavior

Beyond the health risks directly attributed to tattoos and piercings, several studies suggest a possible connection between permanent body art and other types of risk taking among adolescents. These behaviors range from sexual activity to substance abuse.

In 2001 researchers at the University of Rochester Medical Center reported a correlation between teenage risky behavior and tattoos. The following year they linked these behaviors to body piercings. The studies included information from a national sample of 6,072 adolescents that was collected in 1995 and 1996. Youths in the study, who were in junior high or high school, ranged in age from eleven to twenty-one. Overall, about 4.5 percent of the youths had tattoos and piercings, with risky behaviors much more prevalent among those with body art than without. For example, girls with body piercings other than pierced ears were twice as likely as other girls to smoke, skip school, or engage in sexual activity. Pierced girls were also three times more likely to have friends who used drugs or alcohol.

A study published in 2002 by the Adolescent Medicine Division of the Naval Medical Center San Diego reported similar findings. This study was based on a fifty-eight-question survey that was offered to teens who came to the center's adolescent clinic. The survey contained questions about eating behavior, violence, drug abuse, sexual behavior, suicide, tattoos, and body piercings.

The study found that participants with tattoos and/or body piercings were more likely to have engaged in risk-taking behaviors, including eating disorders, drug use, sexual activity, and suicide, than those without either. In addition, violence index scores were three times as high in males with tattoos and two times as high in females with body piercings compared with those without tattoos or piercings. Suicide index scores were nearly twice as high in females with tattoos than those without.

Researchers are unsure whether the link between tattoos, piercings, and risky behavior exists because teenagers who already engage in risky behavior get tattooed and pierced or if teenagers get tattoos and body piercings and then become engaged in risky behavior. Either way, doctors believe that health professionals who see adolescents should take into consideration whether or not they have tattoos and piercings. According to the San Diego study:

> The results from the present study are clear. Adolescents possessing at least one tattoo/piercing have significantly greater risk or degrees of involvement in the areas of drug abuse, sexual activity, disordered eating behaviors, and suicide compared with their peers without tattoo/piercing. The presence of tattoos and body piercings in adolescents does not necessarily indicate risk-taking behavior in particular individuals, however asking questions about these types of risk-taking behaviors should be a part of every adolescent health visit.[27]

Industry Actions

The risks associated with piercings and tattoos have resulted in body art industries taking actions to protect their clients. For example, professional associations provide safety training to tattoo artists and piercers. This training includes recommendations on the safest way to tattoo and pierce, such as strict hygienic procedures that reduce clients' risks of contracting bloodborne diseases and other infections. These

organizations also provide information, via their Web sites and pamphlets, to the general public on how to choose a safe tattoo artist or body piercer.

The Alliance of Professional Tattooists (APT), a professional association of tattoo artists, recommends that people make sure that their tattoo artist uses an autoclave, a machine that uses a combination of heat, steam, and pressure to kill all pathogenic microorganisms. An autoclave should be used to clean equipment after each tattoo. Tattooists should also use gloves when working on a client. The APT Web site also gives specific guidance on what clients should look for to ensure that a tattoo studio is taking steps to reduce infection risks:

> All equipment should be single service. This means that each needle and tube set is individually packaged, dated and sealed and autoclaved. The artist should open a fresh set of needles and tubes in front of you. Any ointments, pigments, needles, gloves, razors, plastic trays or containers used in applying your new tattoo are discarded after use. After the tattoo application, the artist will disinfect the work area with an EPA approved virucidal that will kill any surface bacteria or viruses.[28]

A professional piercer must follow stringent hygiene rules in order to reduce the risk of infection in clients like this woman with multiple piercings.

Like tattoo organizations, professional piercing organizations require that piercers follow strict hygiene rules and provide suggestions to potential clients. The Association of Professional Piercers (APP) recommends that those training to become professional piercers attend a bloodborne pathogens training class from an organization such as the Red Cross or the National Safety Council. The APP also recommends that its members wear gloves when piercing, use autoclave equipment, and use fresh needles with each client. The APP strongly advises the public against getting pierced with a piercing gun. A piercing gun can never be fully sterilized because not all parts of the gun can be removed and autoclaved.

Risk Reducers

To avoid allergic reactions, people with body piercings should only insert jewelry made from high-grade metals.

In addition to choosing a body art professional who follows strict hygienic procedures, people can reduce the health risks associated with body piercing and tattooing by following doctors' recommendations. If a person is taking a blood-thinning

medicine, doctors recommend that the person wait until he or she is off the medicine before getting tattooed or pierced. Doctors also recommend that people with congenital heart disease take antibiotics before getting pierced in order to reduce the risk of contracting endocarditis.

If a person is susceptible to dye allergies, he or she can ask the tattoo artist to do a patch test. This involves having a small amount of ink punched under the skin to see how the body reacts. To avoid allergic reactions to piercings, people should make sure that their piercers insert jewelry made only of the highest grade of stainless steel, niobium, or titanium, the least reactive of jewelry metals.

Body piercing and tattoo professionals also stress that another important way to minimize potential health problems is to follow aftercare instructions. Tattoo professionals recommend that a person leave the bandage on a new tattoo from four hours to overnight, depending on the size of the tattoo. After the bandage is removed, they recommend washing the tattoo gently with a soap that is free of deodorants, skin softeners, or other additives; pat the tattoo dry with a soft towel; and apply a coating of ointment. For the following two weeks, people should not rub, pick, or scratch their new tattoos.

The APP Web site explains how to care for piercings during their healing periods. A person should clean the piercing two to three times daily. The APP recommends that a person first wash his or her hands before cleaning the piercing and then soak the piercing by inverting a cup of warm saline solution over it. Disposable paper products, such as paper towels, are recommended for drying the piercing. During the healing period, the APP recommends that people wear loose clothing over their piercing and keep in the initial jewelry.

By choosing a piercer or tattoo artist who follows strict hygienic procedures and properly following aftercare recommendations, people can greatly reduce their risk of health problems resulting from permanent body art. However, health professionals stress that the health risks of getting tattooed or pierced can never be completely eliminated.

4

Legal Issues

ON DECEMBER 21, 2004, the Medford, Massachusetts, City Council voted to deny Cheryl Voigt a permit to open Lucky's Tattoo in downtown Medford. Councilor Paul Camuso stated that the council members rejected the permit because they were concerned about potential parking problems. Another concern was that the disposal of Lucky's Tattoo's medical waste could endanger children at the Medford Boys and Girls Club, located across the street from the proposed tattoo studio location.

Supporters of Voigt believe that the council had no right to deny the opening of Lucky's Tattoo since tattooing is legal in Massachusetts. They believe that Voigt's permit was actually rejected because the community did not want a tattoo parlor in Medford Square. Voigt reacted to the decision by stating that she would sue the city.

Every day, professional tattoo artists and body piercers like Voigt deal with legal issues such as applying for licenses to open studios. Moreover, body art professionals must abide by state piercing and tattooing regulations, protect themselves from lawsuits, and protect their work from being copied by other body art professionals. Tattoo and piercing clients also are involved in legal issues. Client issues range from understanding how to legally obtain a tattoo or piercing to determining what legal actions are available if someone receives an unsatisfactory tattoo or piercing.

State Laws

No federal laws oversee the tattoo or body piercing industries. Instead, tattoo artists and body piercers must adhere to laws and regulations set by states and cities. Most states require that tattoo artists and body piercers obtain licenses in order to legally operate their businesses. To receive a license, piercers and tattooists must pay fees and adhere to state-specific regulations. One common regulation is that piercers and tattoo artists must obtain a specific amount of training in their field. For example, in Alaska body piercers

The owners of tattoo parlors such as this one must adhere to stringent state and city laws in order to operate.

Under the laws of many states, tattoo artists must complete a set number of hours of training before obtaining a license.

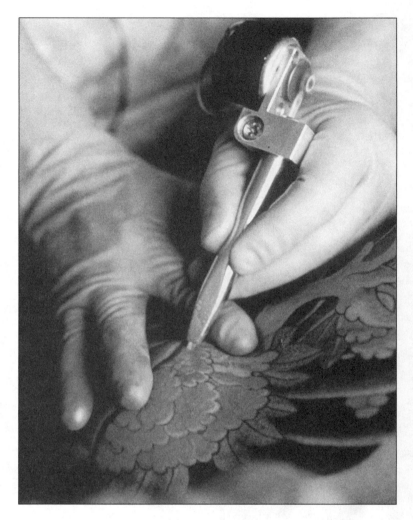

must submit certified copies of student records verifying completion of 1,000 hours of training. Tattoo artists in Alaska must prove that they have completed 380 hours of training.

Professional piercers and tattoo artists must follow additional regulations in order to retain their licenses. State laws often prohibit tattoo artists and piercers from accepting certain people as clients. As an example, Texas law stipulates that tattoo artists and piercers must turn away people who appear to be under the influence of alcohol or drugs. Most states also have age restrictions. In Maine it is illegal for tattoo artists to accept clients under age eighteen. Other states, such as Texas, allow minors to get tattoos or piercings with parental permission.

Health and Safety Requirements

Certain states also require that tattoo artists and body piercers follow specific health regulations. For example, in Virginia people cannot tattoo or perform body piercing on any client unless the tattoo artist or piercer complies with the CDC's guidelines for "Universal Blood and Body Fluid Precautions." Virginia tattoo artists and body piercers must also provide their clients with information about the potential health risks of tattooing and piercing. In states such as Arkansas, tattoo artists must pass a written examination that ensures that the applicant has knowledge of bacteriology and the proper technique needed to reduce the chance of infections and contagious diseases being spread.

Many states require that tattoo and piercing studios follow strict sanitation and hygiene practices as another way to reduce the risk of infections. For example, in Hawaii tattoo studios must provide a sink for the exclusive use of the tattoo artist to wash his or her hands and prepare the customers for tattooing. In Utah tattoo establishments must ensure that all instruments to be used in tattooing, except for plastic stencils, are wrapped in surgical linen wrappers and sterilized by an autoclave for at least thirty minutes.

For safety reasons, some states also place stipulations on where tattoo artists can place tattoos. In Maine and Rhode Island tattoos cannot legally be placed on a person's hands, feet, or above the neck. One of the reasons cited for these restrictions is that tattooing on these body parts increases health risks for the clients.

Reaction to Regulations

Professional body piercers and tattoo artists have varying opinions on state laws and regulations. Although many agree that laws and regulations are needed to legitimize their profession and provide safety for their clients, others feel that certain laws are too restrictive. Laws regarding minors are among the most controversial of the regulations.

Shannon Larratt, editor and publisher of *Body Modification Ezine,* believes that minor laws are often a step toward banning youths from getting body art. He writes:

> It's too easy to allow politicians to force into place high age restrictions as a shallow cover for an attempt to ban and keep piercings out of schools and so on. We allow youths to sign for surgery and drive at sixteen. We allow youths to sign for abortions without parental consent at as young as fourteen. We allow marriage and sex at sixteen in most areas, and we even allow firearms to be owned by teens. . . . If we are then to restrict piercing to eighteen, we need to justify how piercing is more dangerous than these acts and why comprehending them is out of the range of a young person's ability. [29]

Some tattoo artists are concerned that state legislatures are working to restrict tattooing to certain body parts, making full-body art illegal.

Body piercers and tattoo artists are more supportive of hygiene and safety laws than they are of minor laws. They have been instrumental in helping to pass laws that oversee their industries. For example, in the 1970s, Lyle Tuttle, a professional tattoo artist, helped establish tattoo business health code requirements in California. Currently, Mike Wicks, owner of Uncle Freaky's Tattoo and Piercing in Deaver, Wyoming, is pushing to introduce legislation that would establish a minimum health standard for tattoo artists and parlors in his state. Piercers and tattoo artists like Tuttle and Wicks believe that these regulations will establish piercing and tattooing as safe activities and result in more business.

However, body piercers and tattoo artists do not agree with all proposed safety and health regulations. In 2004 the Tattoo, Body-Piercing, and Corrective Cosmetic Artists Act was proposed in Pennsylvania. According to lawmakers, the act's purpose is to provide needed safety and health regulations. Included in this act is a ban on facial tattoos by tattoo artists, although micropigmentation of the face would still be allowed. Body art professionals such as Shannon Larratt regard this as a violation of people's freedom to express themselves. He explains:

> Clearly restricting tattooing to only certain parts of the body is entirely motivated by cultural reasoning, not by safety concerns. The inclusion of this restriction effectively reduces the bill to nonsense. Allowing permanent makeup to be tattooed—where society chooses the artwork by seeking out this year's "normal"—but banning art chosen by the wearer as an individual, is clearly contrary to not only the declared purpose of the bill, but to free speech and expression in general.[30]

Tattoo Bans

Certain states and cities ban not only facial tattooing but all tattooing. Until recently, the states of Maine, South Carolina, and Oklahoma completely banned tattooing. By 2004, Oklahoma remained the only state with a ban still in place.

Oklahoma government representatives give several reasons for the state's tattoo ban. Oklahoma representative Bill Graves believes that it is morally wrong to mark up a

Some states ban facial tattoos, citing health concerns. Tattoo artists condemn such a restriction as an infringement on the individual's right to free expression.

person's body. And he believes that children should be protected from making irreversible mistakes, such as getting a tattoo, that they will be unhappy with later in life. Another reason commonly cited by opponents is the belief that tattooing is a health risk and can lead to the spread of infectious diseases.

Tattoo artists disagree, arguing that tattooing is safe when strict hygienic procedures are followed. Moreover, tattoo artists argue that Oklahoma's ban is hypocritical. Although tattooing is banned, micropigmentation, the tattooing of permanent makeup, is allowed. Both micropigmentation and tattooing use the same machine and are essentially the same procedure.

As a result of the arguments of tattoo artists and their supporters, Oklahoma legislators have considered lifting the ban. In March 2004 the Oklahoma Senate approved a bill to legalize tattooing in the state. If the Oklahoma House also approves the bill, then tattooing will become legal there.

South Carolina's Ban

Until 2004, South Carolina, like Oklahoma, banned tattooing, but professional tattoo artist Ronald White challenged the ban and eventually gained enough supporters to make tattooing legal in his state. He began his fight in 1999 when he tattooed a person in his own home, videotaped the process, and broadcast it to a local television audience. This led to his arrest and a fine of $2,500.

Following the arrest, White admitted to violating the state ban, but took his case to court, claiming that the ban violated his First Amendment right of free expression. In 2002 the South Carolina Supreme Court disagreed with White's argument and stated that the state's concerns about tattooing's health risks outweighed White's First Amendment rights.

White fought on and eventually appealed his conviction to the U.S. Supreme Court. The Center for Individual Freedom (CFIF) filed a brief in support of White's petition. "For the Center, an individual's right to artistic expression is protected without regard to the medium employed or message conveyed by the artist," states the CFIF Web site.

> It matters little to the First Amendment that some people choose art created and sold in tattoo parlors rather than at [art auction houses] Sotheby's or Christie's. Furthermore, while a state has the right to protect the health and safety of its citizens, banning an entire art form, when less restrictive means can adequately safeguard the public, indiscriminately tramples the freedom of artistic expression embodied in the First Amendment.[31]

White also argued that the ban actually increased health risks because many people in South Carolina obtained tattoos illegally in unsanitary conditions and from artists who were not sterilizing equipment. If the tattoo industry was legal and regulated, White contended, tattoo artists would be required to follow hygienic laws that would reduce tattooing health risks.

Ending the Ban

Despite these arguments, the Supreme Court would not hear White's case. White then sued the state of South Carolina, but his case was dismissed. However, his efforts to overturn the ban helped gain supporters, including government representatives.

In 2004 as a result of the increasing numbers of people calling for the legalization of tattooing in South Carolina, the

To avoid laws prohibiting minors from getting tattoos, a majority of adolescents wanting body art seek out amateurs, who work with improper tools in unhygienic environments.

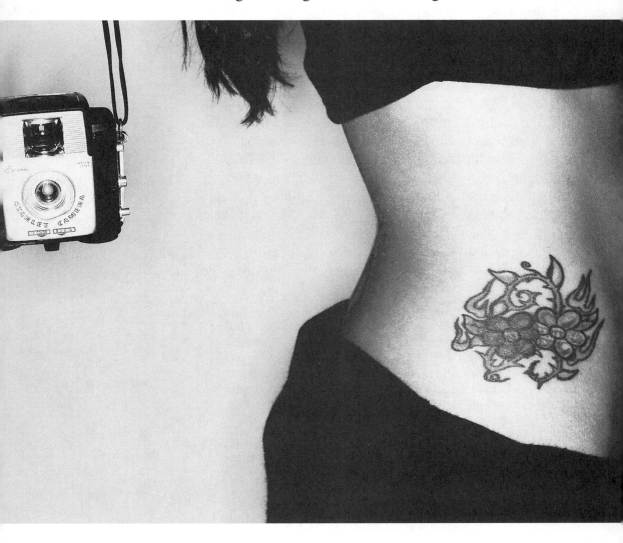

state's general assembly passed a bill that would allow a regulated tattoo industry. The bill required that tattoo artists would not tattoo anyone under age eighteen, and people between the ages of eighteen and twenty-one would be required to obtain parental consent. In addition, the bill banned tattoos above the neck and required tattoo artists to follow local zoning laws and obtain licenses from the health department.

Governor Mark Sanford approved the bill, making it a law. However, he required that the state health department develop health regulations before tattoo artists could open studios. Once the South Carolina Department of Health and Environmental Control determines the state health guidelines and legislators approve them, tattoo entrepreneurs will be able to open for business.

Underground Market

One of the reasons South Carolina representatives voted to end the ban on tattooing was that they were concerned about the growing underground tattoo market. Both state bans and minor laws have led to an increase in illegal piercing and tattooing. The majority of those who get body art illegally are minors.

Teenagers use several methods to get around minor laws. Some turn to "scratchers," unlicensed tattooists or piercers. "Poke and stick" parties, gatherings of teenagers and young adults who pierce and tattoo one another, have also become popular. In addition to avoiding minor laws, teenagers can save money at poke and stick parties. In 2004 Erik Hansen, a twenty-year-old, attended a poke and stick party and got a roughly drawn skull-and-crossbones tattoo on his arm. His friend tattooed it for him using a needle and ink. "It's more fun to have a friend do it—and it was free,"[32] Hansen explained.

Myrna Armstrong, a professor in the School of Nursing at Texas Tech University, completed a body art study involving more than two thousand adolescents in eight states. She found that 54 percent of the adolescents had their body art done by an amateur, using everything from straight pins and sewing needles to pens and pencils.

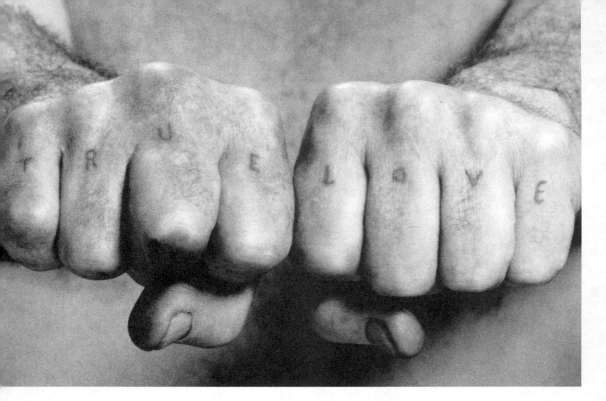

Because unlicensed tattoo artists seldom adhere to hygiene laws, illegal tattoos like this hand art often lead to infection and other health problems.

Unprofessional Results

Illegal piercings and tattoos have resulted in young people getting infections and experiencing other health problems. This is because unlicensed piercers and tattooists often do not follow the hygiene and sanitation laws required of professionals. Scratchers or piercers and tattooists at poke and stick parties often do not sterilize their equipment or use fresh needles with each person.

A recent example of the perils of unhygienic tattoo practices occurred in Colerain, Ohio. In May 2004 two Colerain high school students became sick after visiting an apartment that housed an unlicensed tattoo and body piercing studio. At least 150 students from four area high schools were estimated to have visited the apartment for tongue piercings and tattoos. Police found the studio's sterilization procedures to be lax. Health officials advised the students to see a doctor about possible exposure to hepatitis B, hepatitis C, and HIV.

Police throughout the country are cracking down on illegal piercing and tattooing because of the health risks. For example, Tony Pippin, who lived at the apartment in Colerain where the piercings and tattoos were done, was arrested. He faced misdemeanor charges for running an unlicensed tattoo or body piercing business and doing procedures without parental consent.

Minors have also faced charges for giving their peers tattoos and piercings. In June 2004 Oneonta, New York, state police charged Reaves A. Kimbel, age seventeen, with two counts of unlawfully dealing with a child. It is illegal to tattoo anyone under eighteen in New York. Kimbel allegedly gave tattoos to a fourteen-year-old and a fifteen-year-old.

Equipment in this licensed tattoo studio is properly maintained in accordance with state laws, reducing the risk of infection to its clients.

As a result of these legal issues, some professional piercers and tattoo artists have implemented rules that are even stricter than their state laws. For example, in Wyoming minors are allowed to get tattoos if they have parental consent. Even so, tattoo artist Mike Wicks refuses to tattoo anyone under age sixteen. He will tattoo minors age sixteen and over only if both they and their parents bring a photo ID, sign forms of consent, and answer questions regarding intoxication, pregnancy, and diseases.

Unhappy Clients

Even professional body piercers and tattoo artists who follow the law can become involved in legal problems. These problems often involve dissatisfied customers. Certain clients feel that the tattoos or piercings they received are not what they expected. Some of these clients blame the tattoo artists or piercers for poor-quality work and sue for damages.

In 1999, for example, Lee Williams of Roseville, Michigan, sued Eternal Tattoos for $25,000 after getting a tattoo from the studio. Williams requested that the word *villain* be tattooed on his right forearm. However, neither he nor the tattoo artist knew how to correctly spell the word. The tattoo artist decided the word was spelled "villian," and Williams agreed with this decision. Only after getting the tattoo did Williams discover the word was misspelled. Although he agreed to the spelling, Williams believed Eternal Tattoos was at fault and sued for damages.

Other tattoo artists have been sued because they have used their clients' tattoos to gain publicity. For example, Greg Ashcraft of Skinworx Tattoo in Bessemer, Alabama, was sued in 2002 by a client for submitting photos of her and her tattoo to a national body art magazine, allegedly without her consent. At that time, a judge dismissed the case, stating that it was not an invasion of privacy. Wendy Minnifield, another client, sued Ashcraft for the same reason in December 2004. This time a state appeals court determined that submitting a photo of Minnifield to a magazine without her permission was a breach of ethics. The suit is ongoing.

Protecting Work

Other issues that arise in the body art industry involve copyright laws. As custom tattoos have become more common, tattoo professionals are finding that they need to protect their work from being copied by others. To do so, they can register their work with the U.S. Copyright Office. A tattoo artist who illegally copies a copyrighted tattoo can be sued for damages by the original artist.

Despite the fact that a copyright would protect their work, not all body artists believe that copyrighting is a good idea. Certain body art professionals, such as tattooist Pat Fish, believe that the industry should self-regulate because having outsiders, such as lawyers, interfere could result in an atmosphere of distrust. Nevertheless, other body artists believe that copyrighting custom work is a positive step for the body art industry because it shows that society recognizes tattoos as an art form.

As the body art community continues to debate whether or not to employ copyrights, some have already put copyrights to use. Artists who create flash, tattoo design sheets, own the copyright to their work at creation. The creator sells licenses to tattoo artists that allow them to use the designs in their tattoos. Buyers of flash may resell their own copies of the flash, but they are not allowed to make copies of the sheets and sell or exchange them. Doing so would be copyright infringement.

An example of a copyright infringement case relating to tattoos recently occurred in Portland, Oregon. Matthew Reed of TigerLilly Tattoo and Design Works is suing to stop Detroit Pistons player Rasheed Wallace from displaying his tattoo in an ad for Nike basketball shoes. In 1998 Wallace approached Reed because he wanted a tattoo of an Egyptian-themed family with a king, queen, and three children. Reed researched the idea and created a custom design, which he tattooed onto Wallace's arm. Reed claims that displaying this tattoo in the ad is a violation of the copyright he owns for a pencil drawing of an Egyptian family. Wallace claims that since he approached Reed with the idea for the design, either he owns the intellectual property

A tattoo artist traces a scorpion design from a collection of licensed artwork. Many tattoo designs are copyrighted and can only be reproduced under license.

rights to the design or shares them with Reed. If a court determines that Reed and Wallace share ownership, Reed says he is entitled to part of the money that Wallace was paid for the ad, which ran on television and on the Internet.

Government Protection in Use

Although Reed has a copyright of his pencil drawing used for Wallace's tattoo, to date no one has sought a copyright for an actual custom-designed tattoo. However, in November 2002 Elayne Angel, master piercer and owner of the Rings of Desire body piercing specialty studio, received a service mark, another form of government protection, for her tattoo design of black and gray angel wings. Angel worked with tattoo artist Bob Roberts to create the design, then Roberts tattooed the wings onto Angel in 1987. Angel's service mark, a government registration to protect a symbol used in the sale or advertising of services of one company from those of others, protects her wings from being used in advertisements by other piercing studios.

Angel believes that government registration of body art is necessary to protect people's custom work. "I think it is totally fair for original artwork of all kinds to be copyrighted, including tattoos. I have to say, even though imitation is considered a form of flattery, it really freaks me out to see my wings tattooed on other people!" Angel states. "They are an original, very personal artwork. They were designed by the artist, and myself, working together to create the design that was perfect for me. The idea that someone saw a picture, and brought it to an artist to be copied, shocks and disturbs me!"[33]

Professional body art organizations, such as the Association of Professional Piercers, supported Angel's decision. After Angel's wings received a service mark, the APP stated in its newsletter, "By agreeing to register a tattoo, the U.S. Patent and Trademark Office has indicated that the products of our studios are indeed commercial artwork and worthy of legal protection. A tattoo can now be afforded the same consideration granted a piece of poetry, music or art used in the business world. Having this legal precedent on our side serves to further establish body art as a profession in the eyes of the law."[34]

5

Removing Body Art

THE INCREASING NUMBER of people getting tattooed or pierced has led to a rise in people wanting to rid themselves of their body art. A 2003 Harris Poll found that 17 percent of Americans wish they had not gotten their tattoos. Americans are not the only ones unhappy with their body art decisions. According to a study by the *British Journal of Dermatology,* in the United Kingdom 75 percent of tattooed people regret their decision to get inked.

People regret their body art for many reasons. Some claim that their body piercings negatively impact their careers; others are unhappy when their tattoos fade and distort over time. Those no longer satisfied with their body art have several options, many of them painful and expensive, to rid themselves of their piercings and tattoos. These options range from covering their piercings with clothing to surgically removing their tattoos.

Professional Problems

One of the more common problems people experience with body art is that it negatively affects their careers. Today, more companies allow their employees to openly display tattoos and piercings than they did in the past. Despite this fact, an employee's chances of moving ahead are often diminished because of his or her body art.

According to Cindy Graf, director of the Laser Centers of Wisconsin, a facility that removes tattoos, tattoos have found a certain level of acceptance in industries such as fashion, beauty, and retail. However, in her experience, tattoos in a professional business setting are less acceptable. Those involved in the job placement industry agree with Graf's assessment. "People who want to be promoted and be successful abandon [the tattoos and piercings] pretty quickly," said Carol Schneider, CEO of SEEK, Incorporated. Such adornments "may hold people back," she added, noting that "the people in positions of power are pretty conservative. If a person wants to join the ranks of power, they need to dress appropriately."[35]

A 2001 survey by Vault.com, an online management site, backs this viewpoint. Of the five hundred participants questioned in the survey, 18 percent of tattooed or pierced employees and 24 percent of tattooed or pierced managers said that their tattoos or piercings have hindered their career prospects. In addition, 42 percent of managers said they would lower their opinion of someone based on his or her tattoos or body piercings, and 10 percent said they had had to discipline workers because of tattoos or piercings. Managers

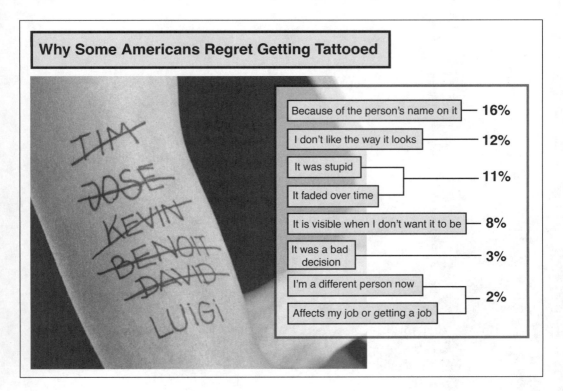

Why Some Americans Regret Getting Tattooed

Reason	Percent
Because of the person's name on it	16%
I don't like the way it looks	12%
It was stupid / It faded over time	11%
It is visible when I don't want it to be	8%
It was a bad decision	3%
I'm a different person now / Affects my job or getting a job	2%

also stated that tattoos or piercings may negatively affect a person's ability to get a job: 58 percent said they would be less likely to offer a job to a tattooed or pierced applicant.

On the Job

Even if a person with a visible tattoo or piercing is accepted at a job, he or she often has to deal with dress codes that discourage body art. Because of the increasing number of people sporting body art, several companies have instituted strict dress codes regarding piercings and tattoos. Companies have these dress code policies because they want their employees to appear professional when dealing with customers. For example, Starbucks workers cannot display any tattoos or wear any piercing jewelry besides small, matched

A heavily tattooed man pulls up data on the computer for his boss. Many companies prohibit their employees from displaying body art in the workplace.

earrings, and each employee's ear cannot have more than two piercings.

Stricter rules are enforced at Disney theme parks. None of the fifty-six thousand employees at the Magic Kingdom, Epcot Center, MGM Studios, or Disney's Animal Kingdom can wear piercings or visible tattoos. "We feel that the appearance guidelines reflect the appearance and quality and the attention to detail that Disney wants to project as a professional company, and those are guidelines that Disney guests have come to expect,"[36] said Rene Callahan, a Disney spokeswoman.

Even professional sports, in which tattoos and piercings are common, have limits as to what body art players are allowed to display. For example, the San Francisco–area Webcor cycling team has told team member David Clinger that he must remove his face-and-scalp tattoo or stop riding. Team officials are concerned that Clinger's tattoo could upset team sponsors such as Webcor Builders, PowerBar, and Nike Cycling. Clinger has begun laser treatments to start the removal process, but it could take months of treatments to remove the tattoo. Team managers must decide whether Clinger will be allowed to race while the treatments are ongoing or if he will be sidelined until the tattoo is completely gone.

Religious Issues

Another reason people regret their piercings and tattoos is the negative response from their religious associations. Certain Christian sects believe that it is morally wrong to get tattooed or pierced. They believe that the body is a gift from God and should not be desecrated. This view is based on Leviticus 19:28 of the Bible, which states, "You shall not make any cuttings in your flesh for the dead, nor tattoo any marks upon you: I am the Lord."

Other Christians believe that the act of getting body art is not necessarily a sin, but the reason a person gets a tattoo or piercing may be against the church's beliefs. For example, the Catholic Church does not forbid body modifications. However, church leaders do believe that if a person gets a tattoo or piercing as a way to rebel against his or her parents or other people, the action is not in the spirit of Jesus Christ and the teaching of the church.

In addition to Christians, many Jewish people believe that the practice of tattooing or piercing is in violation of Leviticus 19:28, which is part of the Torah, the books of Jewish law. When comparing tattooing and piercing to cosmetic surgery, Rabbi Mark Washofsky writes, "Tattooing and more extreme forms of body piercing, when not undertaken as part of a regimen of medicine or reconstructive surgery, are most difficult to reconcile with Jewish tradition, which commands us to strive for holiness and to treat our bodies with reverence and respect."[37]

Growing Older

The changes associated with getting older also result in people regretting their tattoos or piercings. Body art changes in appearance over the years. Tattoos can become faded after years of sun exposure. According to a 2003 Harris Poll, the third most common reason people regretted their tattoos is that their tattoos had faded. Also, if a tattoo artist injects the pigments too deeply into the skin, the pigments may migrate beyond the original tattoo sites, resulting in a blurred appearance over time.

Piercings change over time as well. Jewelry can migrate, or travel through the skin, and settle in a different position from the original piercing. As it migrates, the jewelry may make the piercing larger. In this case, if the jewelry is not removed, it will continue to migrate until it creates a hole large enough for the jewelry to fall out. Once this happens, the possibility of getting scars from the piercing is likely.

A person's physical changes can also affect his or her body art. Tattoos can stretch if a person gains weight. This is one reason why doctors suggest teenagers wait until their body has completely grown before getting a tattoo. Piercings are also affected by body changes. For example, pregnant women with navel piercings may find that their abdomens expand to the point that their navels protrude and the jewelry is pushed off.

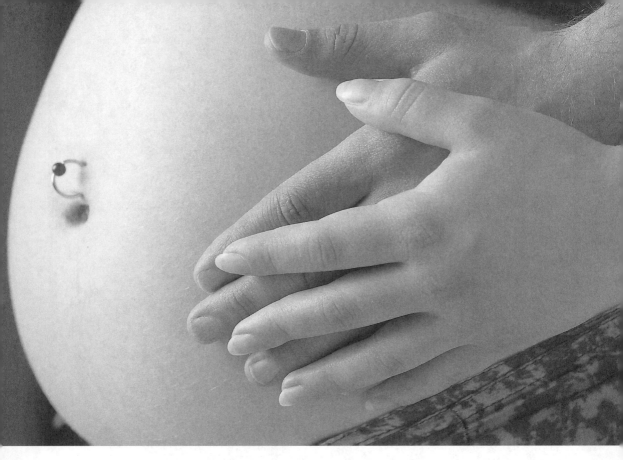

Another reason people become unhappy with their body art is that their attitudes and taste often change over the years. What may have seemed "cool" at age eighteen may look silly or not reflect someone's lifestyle years later. At age twenty-one, Rachod Mildton of Lansing, Michigan, had a devil's face tattooed beneath his left eye. "I was a different person back then. . . . I was with the wrong crowd, abusing alcohol and hanging out in the streets," Mildton, now twenty-seven, explained. "I have to be a positive role model for my daughters. . . . The tattoo is not a representation of the person I am now."[38]

This pregnant woman's abdomen may grow so large that it will push out her navel jewelry.

Gang Tattoo Regrets

Former gang members are often among those who feel that their tattoos no longer represent their current lifestyle. Their tattoos remind them of their past, often violent, life. Moreover, gang tattoos can negatively affect a former member's chances of getting a job and how other people perceive him or her.

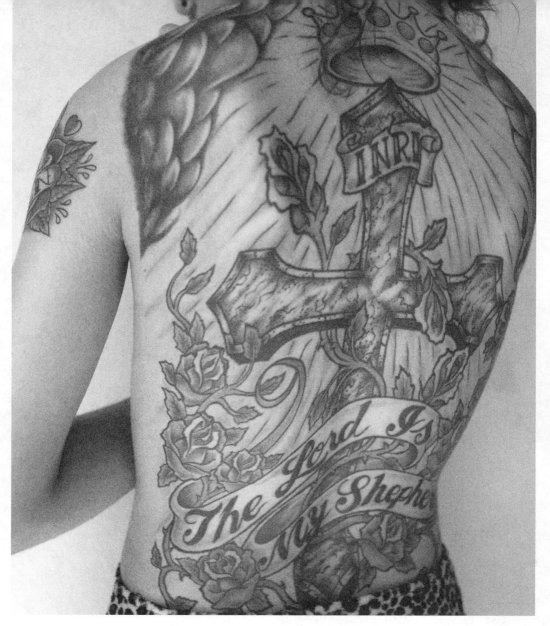

This woman with a large cross and other tattoos across her back may regret her body art as she gets older.

Emerson Javier Sanchez experienced these effects. Sanchez joined a gang at age thirteen and became involved in violent activities and drugs. When Sanchez was sixteen, he decided to get his gang nickname tattooed onto his neck. At age twenty-five, however, Sanchez was no longer in a gang and was living a completely different life than that of his teenage years. He was attending college with the goal of either studying abnormal psychology or becoming a writer.

After having changed his life, Sanchez longed to get rid of the tattoo and everything it symbolized. However, tattoo removal is an expensive process and for years Sanchez could not afford to do it.

Removal Programs

The San Mateo Tattoo Removal program, which is funded and organized by the San Mateo, California, Juvenile Hall, gave Sanchez a chance to get rid of the last remnant of his old life. To qualify for free tattoo removal, ex–gang members must first complete twenty hours of community service. Then they go through the long process of having their tattoos removed. In 2001 Sanchez began this process.

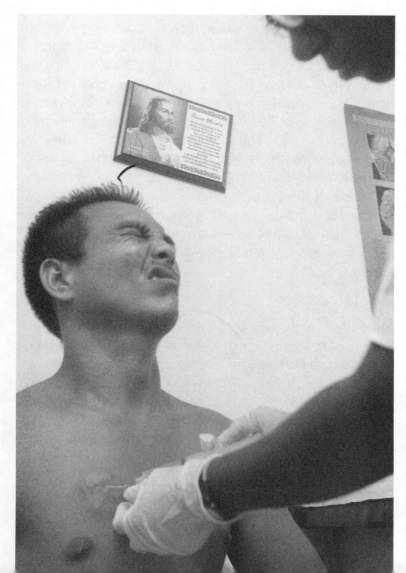

A former gang member begins the painful process of tattoo removal. Gang members who mend their ways typically regret their tattoos.

Sanchez started to get laser treatments to have his tattoo removed and, after two years, completed his treatments in 2003. Although the process was long and painful, he was happy to get rid of the tattoo. "I feel much better now because I don't feel like I'm stereotyped when I go places anymore," Sanchez stated. "Everything it symbolizes is not in my life anymore."[39]

Gang tattoo removal programs like San Mateo's are becoming more common nationwide. Police departments run many of the programs. For example, in August 2004 the police department in Wichita, Kansas, created Operation Fresh Start. Former gang members can have their tattoos removed in exchange for an allotment of community service and $25 to pay for the anesthetic used during the removal process. The police officers believe the service helps the community as well as former gang members because it reduces the chances that they will return to their old lifestyle.

In addition to police departments, nonprofit groups have started gang tattoo removal programs. Agape Light provides services for troubled and low-income persons, including tattoo removal, antigang counseling, family counseling, and spiritual direction. It offers tattoo removal to people coming out of prison who want to remove their tattoos and reenter mainstream society. Currently the organization exists in Southern California, but there are plans to expand it nationwide.

Breakups

Other life changes that lead to body art regrets include divorces and breakups. Relationship tattoos, tattoos of a loved one's name, have surged in popularity over the past decade. However, people who get relationship tattoos and then break up with their loved ones typically want to rid themselves of such tattoos.

This has been true of several celebrities. For example, socialite Paris Hilton's former boyfriend, pop singer Nick Carter, put her name on his wrist in July 2004. About three weeks later, they broke up. In January 2005 Carter got a skull-and-crossbones tattoo to cover up the "Paris" tattoo.

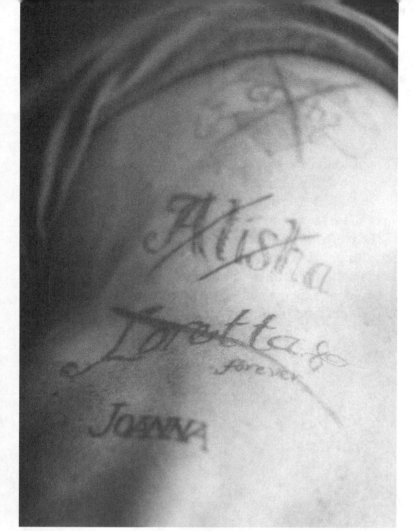

A tattoo of an ex-lover's name makes an unpleasant souvenir of a broken relationship, as this man's arm shows.

Actor Johnny Depp's right upper arm used to display a tattoo of "Winona Forever" in honor of his relationship with actress Winona Ryder. However, their love did not last. In 1993 this tattoo was laser-edited into "Wino Forever" following the couple's breakup.

Like celebrities, many ordinary people with relationship tattoos come to regret their decisions. A 2003 Harris Poll found that the most common reason a person regrets a tattoo is that a person's name is in the tattoo. As a result, dermatologists and plastic surgeons are receiving more tattoo removal work. "The number of tattoos people are getting removed is increasing," says Jeffrey Rockmore, a plastic surgeon with the Plastic Surgery Group in Albany. "Years ago, there was a big wave in tattoos and those relationships ended so people want to get rid of the evidence."[40]

Removal Methods

When a person wants to remove unwanted body art, his or her options depend on whether the art is a piercing or tattoo. There is only one method to remove a piercing. A person can remove the jewelry and typically the hole will close. However, bad scarring can result from the piercings. To get rid of these scars, a person may require plastic surgery.

There are several options to choose from if a person decides to get rid of an unwanted tattoo. However, most of these methods are time-consuming, expensive, and painful. To avoid the expense and pain, some people decide to cover up their old tattoos with new ones.

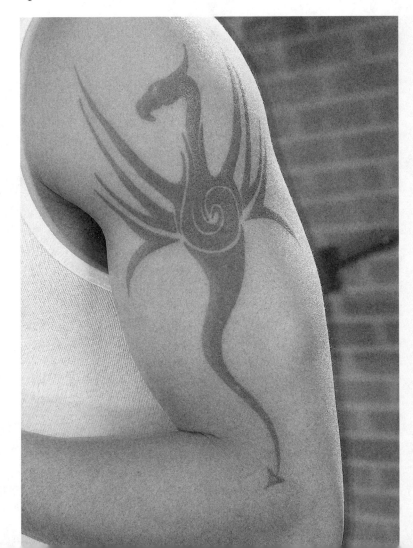

Some people avoid the pain and expense of tattoo removal by incorporating an old tattoo into a new design.

Although a cover-up has advantages over removing unwanted tattoos, it can be technically involved. One method is to first cover the old tattoo with a flesh-colored pigment. This does not completely cover the tattoo because flesh colors do not blend completely with human skin. However, this method gives the tattoo artist a cleaner slate to work with before inking a new tattoo over the old one.

Another method is to ink right over the old tattoo with a new tattoo. The more complex a tattoo is, the more difficult this method is. According to author Jean-Chris Miller, "A good tattooist maps out the colors and lines of your existing tattoo and then designs a new piece that corresponds to the old one. For example, if your old tattoo had brown on top and yellow at the bottom, the new one—while being a completely different design—will also have to be dark on top and a darker color on the bottom. The reason is that you can't cover dark pigment with a lighter pigment."[41] Tribal design tattoos are often used to cover up old tattoos. Tribal tattoos are typically done in black ink and abstract so they can be shaped to cover up most tattoos.

Several well-known celebrities have used the cover-up method. After his marriage with actress Angelina Jolie failed, actor Billy Bob Thornton covered up the tattoo of her name, which was on his left forearm, with an angel and the word *Peace*. When actress Pamela Anderson split from rocker husband Tommy Lee, she had the tattoo around her finger that read "Tommy" changed to "Mommy."

More Options

Despite the relative ease of covering up an old tattoo, many people want them completely removed. Spectrum Consulting estimates that in 1996, 275,000 Americans had their tattoos removed by a medical procedure. One of the less invasive medical procedures available is acid skin peels.

Acid skin peels burn off layers of skin with chemicals, eventually fading the tattoo. This method does not require a visit to a doctor. A tattooed person can purchase an acid peel directly from a company and apply it at home. The major disadvantage of acid skin peels is that their effectiveness is uncertain.

Excision is another tattoo removal option. This process is technically involved and requires surgery. First the tattooed area is numbed with a local anesthetic. Then the tattoo is removed with a scalpel. Next, the skin edges are brought together and sutured. Using this procedure, smaller tattoos can be completely removed in one session. Large tattoos, however, often require more than one surgery. A skin graft might also be needed from another part of the body to close up the incision. This surgical technique always leaves a line scar that can potentially spread.

Dermabrasion is another surgical removal method. The dermabrasion process involves freezing the tattooed area with a surface refrigerant. The tattoo is then sanded off with a rotating instrument. The top layers of skin are scraped away to remove the pigmented skin and encourage the growth of a new layer of skin. This process can typically be completed in one treatment session. However, this technique does not work as well on amateur tattoos as it does on professional tattoos. This is because most amateur tattoos are applied at varying depths, so the surgeon who administers the dermabrasion treatment might not be able to remove all of the pigment deposits. Scarring and pigment abnormalities are common side effects of this process.

Laser Removal

Because laser treatment causes few side effects, it has become the most common tattoo removal method. During laser treatment, pulses of laser light pass through the outer skin layer and break up the pigment of the tattoo. The body then flushes out the pigment-filled cells.

One advantage of laser removal is that the risk of scarring is very low. Typically, only 1 to 2 percent of those receiving laser treatment get scars. Also, a person's skin returns to its natural pigment in a few months. Another advantage is that laser treatments are effective at removing any size tattoo. Actress Angelina Jolie used the laser method to erase the name of her ex-husband Billy Bob Thornton.

A disadvantage to laser treatments is that the larger the tattoo is, the more treatments required. Depending on the tattoo's size, a person may require from two to eight sessions, each spaced four to six weeks apart. The sessions are spaced apart so that the body has time to absorb the pigment residue. The treatments typically cost $250 to $850 per session. Removing a large, professional color tattoo could cost thousands of dollars, five times the original cost of the tattoo. Plus, the more treatments a person has, the more damage is done to the skin. Laser treatments can cause painful blisters and scabs. Also, laser treatment does not guarantee that the entire tattoo will be removed. Certain inks are more difficult to remove depending on what type of laser is used. A Ruby laser, for example, has difficulty treating red.

An ex-gang member has a tattoo burned off with laser treatment, a common procedure for tattoo removal.

Alternatives

Many people who get rid of unwanted tattoos or piercings are still interested in sporting body art. There are several alternatives to permanent body art that these people, and those who are unsure if they want to get pierced or tattooed, are turning to. These alternatives include temporary tattoos, fake piercings, and mehndi.

Temporary tattoos initially were famous for being a kid's prize found in a Cracker Jack box. Today they are no longer just for children. Many adults use temporary tattoos to decorate their body for short time periods. Temporary tattoos come in many different designs, some created by tattoo artists. The best-quality temporary tattoos are made on special paper, such as rice paper; are waterproof; and last as long as two weeks.

A new type of temporary tattoo gaining popularity is a hair tattoo. A person can have a symbol, such as a star or dolphin, shaped into his or her hair. The process involves choosing a specially molded design block, which comes in a variety of shapes and sizes, and placing the block onto a hairstyling hot plate. The hot plate is then placed and kept in the hair for at least fifteen minutes for the desired result. Typically the hair tattoo lasts only until the next time the person washes his or her hair, but special gels can help it last longer.

Like temporary and hair tattoos, fake piercings are a way to try body art without pain or permanency. From stick-on nose studs to magnetic earrings, jewelry that simulates piercings are available at a variety of stores. These items are gaining popularity among celebrities. For example, ex–Spice Girl Victoria Beckham donned a clip-on lip ring rather than pierce her lip.

Mehndi, an Indian tradition of decorating a woman's hands and feet with henna dye, is also becoming a popular alternative to permanent tattoos. The patterns are intricate and can take hours to paint. The henna dye lasts from ten days to six weeks, depending on the person's skin. Mehndi shops are opening up across the United States.

Mehndi, fake piercings, and temporary tattoos are becoming common fashion accessories. Their popularity is likely to increase as more people become interested in decorating their bodies but do not want to suffer the potential consequences of permanent tattoos and piercings.

No matter what form of body art, whether temporary or permanent, becomes most popular, many believe that it will continue to be a part of our culture. Miller writes:

> The combination of technology, historical awareness, and artistic ability have taken body art to heights never before imagined. It's exciting to wonder just how far it can evolve. More than part of our past, body art is part of our present and future. [42]

Notes

Introduction

1. Quoted in Kristopher Kaiyala, "The Skin Game: Once 'Graffiti,' Now Body Art," MSNBC.com, November 2, 2004. www.msnbc.msn.com/id/6124648.

2. Margo DeMello, *Bodies of Inscription: A Cultural History of the Modern Tattoo Community.* Durham, NC: Duke University Press, 2000, p. 70.

Chapter 1: Tattoos and Body Piercing Today

3. Quoted in Yasmine Zaki, "Nipple Accessories—Strange or Trendy?" *Daily Helmsman,* February 17, 2004. www.daily helmsman.com/vnews/display.v/ART/2004/02/17/4031a28c33a2e.

4. Quoted in Steel Navel, "SteelNavel.com News," January 2002. www.steelnavel.com/news/body-jewelry-news-02-01.asp.

5. Kelly Luker, "Needle Freaks," *Metro,* July 26–August 1, 2001. www.metroactive.com/papers/metro/07.26.01/cover/tattoo-0130.html.

6. Luker, "Needle Freaks."

7. Rodney Robinson, interview with the author, Norfolk, VA, February 7, 2005.

8. Debra Knickerbocker, interview with the author, Norfolk, VA, January 31, 2005.

9. Clinton Sanders, *Customizing the Body: The Art and Culture of Tattooing.* Philadelphia: Temple University Press, 1989, p. 29.

10. Sanders, *Customizing the Body,* p. 18.

11. Quoted in Charles Booth, "Now, Everybody Gets Tattoos," *Tennessean,* December 31, 2002. www.tennessean.com/local/archives/02/12/27100689.shtml?Element_ID=27100689.

12. Quoted in Caoimhe Young, "A Passion for Piercing; 'Our Clients Range from Teenagers to Teachers,'" (*London*) *Sunday Mirror,* September 27, 1998. http://static.highbeam.com/s/sunday mirrorlondonengland/september271998/apassionforpiercingour clientsrangefromteenagerstot.

Chapter 2: Why Do People Get Body Art?

13. Quoted in V. Vale and Andrea Juno, eds., *Modern Primitives.* San Francisco: Re/Search Publications, 1989, p. 55.

14. Quoted in Sanders, *Customizing the Body,* p. 51.

15. Quoted in Sanders, *Customizing the Body,* p. 43.

16. Quoted in Sanders, *Customizing the Body,* p. 46.

17. Quoted in DeMello, *Bodies of Inscription,* p. 157.

18. Quoted in R. Morgan Griffin, "All About Genital Piercing," 2003. www.bodyjewelry99.com/articles/genitalpiercing.htm.

19. Quoted in Lisa Klassen, "A Piece of Art," *Daily Bruin,* February 6, 2001. www.dailybruin.ucla.edu/db/printer.asp?ID =2790.

20. Jean-Chris Miller, *The Body Art Book: A Complete Illustrated Guide to Tattoos, Piercings, and Other Body Modifications.* New York: Berkley, 1997, p. 36.

21. Quoted in Vale and Juno, *Modern Primitives,* p. 106.

22. Quoted in *Ananova,* "Leopard Man Shuns Society for Hut on Isle of Skye," 2004. www.ananova.com/news/story/sm_435810.html.

23. Kelly Rothenberg, "Tattooed People as Taboo Figures in Modern Society," 1996. www.bmezine.com/tattoo/tattab.html.

Chapter 3: Health Issues

24. Miller, *The Body Art Book,* p. 87.

25. Quoted in Peggy Peck, "Thinking About Getting a Tattoo? Think Again," WebMD, April 9, 2001. http://my.webmd.com/content/article/35/1728_76844.htm.

26. Quoted in American Association of Nurse Anesthetists, "Anesthesia Risks of Tattoos and Pierced Tongues More than

Skin Deep," August 26, 2004. www.aana.com/press/2004/0826 04.asp.

27. Sean T. Carroll, Robert H. Riffenburgh, Timothy A. Roberts, and Elizabeth B. Myhre, "Tattoos and Body Piercings as Indicators of Adolescent Risk-Taking Behaviors," *Pediatrics,* June 2002. http://pediatrics.aappublications.org/cgi/content/full/ 109/6/1021.

28. Alliance of Professional Tattooists, "Frequently Asked Questions." www.safe-tattoos.com/faq.htm.

Chapter 4: Legal Issues

29. Shannon Larratt, "Regulation: Attacks from Within?" *Body Modification Ezine,* June 15, 2003. www.bmezine.com/ news/pubring/20030615.html.

30. Shannon Larratt, "BME Commentary on PA House Bill No. 615," *Body Modification Ezine,* November 9, 2004. www. bmezine.com/news/pubring/20041109.html.

31. Center for Individual Freedom, "The Indelible Right of Free Expression," August 30, 2002. www.cfif.org/htdocs/free domonline/current/in_our_opinion/tattoo_free_speech.html.

32. Quoted in MSNBC, "The Risks of Do-It-Yourself Tattoos," February 25, 2004. www.msnbc.msn.com/id/4370500.

33. Quoted in Marisa Kakoulas, "The Tattoo Copyright Controversy," *Body Modification Ezine,* December 8, 2003. www.bmezine.com/news/guest/20031208.html.

34. Quoted in Kakoulas, "The Tattoo Copyright Controversy."

Chapter 5: Removing Body Art

35. Quoted in Ann Brownfield, "Tattoos and Other Body Adornments Are More Popular than Ever, but They Still Haven't Pierced the Mainstream Business World," *Greater Milwaukee Today,* September 20, 2004. www.gmtoday.com/news/ local_stories/2004/September_04/09202004_04.asp.

36. Quoted in Hans H. Chen, "Tat Tactics: What Companies Think of Your Tattoos," Vault.com, 2001. www.vault.com/nr/ main_article_detail.jsp?article_id=5326114&listelement=2& cat_id=0_&ht_type=5.

37. Mark Washofsky, "Cosmetic Surgery: A Jewish View," MyJewishLearning.com. www.myjewishlearning.com/daily_life/ TheBody/Adorning_the_Body/Cosmetic_Surgery.htm.

38. Quoted in John Schneider, "Woman with Skull Is 'Tattoo Tale' Winner," *Lansing State Journal,* July 30, 2004. www.lsj.com/news/capitol/040730_john_lb.html.

39. Quoted in *Guardsman,* "Skin Deep: Tattoo Removal," October 29, 2003. http://theguardsman.com/20031029/features.html.

40. Quoted in Kristi L. Gustafson, "Relationship Tattoos Surge in Popularity," *Albany Times Union,* August 18, 2004. www.azcentral.com/ent/dating/articles/0818partnerart.html.

41. Miller, *The Body Art Book,* p. 123.

42. Miller, *The Body Art Book,* p. 15.

Glossary

autoclave: A device that sterilizes equipment by heating materials above the boiling point.

bloodborne disease: A disease that is passed by contamination of blood. Examples include HIV, hepatitis B, and hepatitis C.

body piercing: The perforation of any human body part for the purpose of inserting jewelry or other decoration.

branding: The burning of the skin, usually with hot metal, to leave a scar of a design.

copyright: A form of government protection for an original work of authorship.

custom tattoo: A tattoo designed specifically for the client by the tattooist.

dermabrasion: A surgical method to remove tattoos that involves removing the top layers of skin with an electrical machine.

excision: A surgical method to remove tattoos using a scalpel.

flash: Sets of pictures drawn by artists that are distributed to tattoo studios. Customers can choose a design from flash to have tattooed on their bodies.

granuloma: A nodule that forms around material the body perceives as foreign.

keloid: An abnormal proliferation of scar tissue.

laser removal: A method of removing a tattoo by pulsing laser light through the outer skin to break up the tattoo pigments.

mehndi: An Indian tradition of decorating a woman's hands and feet with henna dye.

micropigmentation: The tattooing of permanent makeup, such as eyeliner or lipstick.

modern primitive movement: A movement in which people turn to the rituals, such as piercing and tattooing, of ancient peoples.

poke and stick party: A gathering of teenagers and young adults who pierce and tattoo one another.

scarification: The deliberate cutting of the skin to create scars.

scratcher: An unlicensed tattooist or piercer.

service mark: A government registration to protect a symbol used in the sale or advertising of services of one company from those of others.

tattoo machine: An electric motor that pushes a hollow needle filled with permanent ink in and out of the skin.

Organizations to Contact

Alliance of Professional Tattooists (APT)

2108 S. Alvernon Way
Tucson, AZ 85711
(520) 514-5549
fax: (520) 514-5579
www.safe-tattoos.com

The Alliance of Professional Tattooists is a nonprofit educational organization that was founded in 1992 to address the health and safety issues facing the tattoo industry. Through education, knowledge, and activism, APT and its members promote the understanding that professional tattooing is a safe expression of art. APT holds seminars at tattoo conventions across the country on the prevention of disease transmission in tattooing.

American Academy of Dermatology

1350 I St. NW, Suite 870
Washington, DC 20005-4355
(202) 842-3555
fax: (202) 842-4355
www.aad.org

The American Academy of Dermatology is the largest dermatologic association. With a membership of more than fourteen thousand physicians worldwide, the academy is committed to advancing the diagnosis and medical, surgical, and cosmetic treatment of the skin, hair, and nails. Its Web site includes professional opinions on whether or not tattoos and piercings are safe, in addition to information about removal methods.

American Medical Association (AMA)

515 N. State St.
Chicago, IL 60610
(800) 621-8335
www.ama-assn.org

The AMA's mission is to speak out on issues important to patients' and the nation's health. The AMA, made up of physician delegates representing every state, encourages the state regulation of tattoo artists and tattoo facilities to ensure adequate procedures to protect the public health.

Association of Professional Piercers (APP)

PMB 286 5456 Peachtree Industrial Blvd.
Chamblee, GA 30341
(888) 888-1APP
www.safepiercing.org
email: info@safepiercing.org

The APP is an international nonprofit association dedicated to disseminating vital health and safety information related to body piercing to piercers, health care providers, and the general public. Its Web site contains factual information about body piercing for both body piercers and those getting pierced.

Centers for Disease Control and Prevention (CDC)

1600 Clifton Rd.
Atlanta, GA 30333
(404) 639-3311
www.cdc.gov

The Centers for Disease Control and Prevention is recognized as the leading federal agency for protecting the health and safety of people at home and abroad, providing credible information to enhance health decisions, and promoting health through strong partnerships. The CDC provides information on the potential of contracting infectious diseases through tattooing and piercing and how to mitigate this risk.

Christian Tattoo Association (CTA)

2815 Gull Rd.
Kalamazoo, MI 49048

(269) 998-7738
www.xtat.org
email: freak@xtat.org

The Christian Tattoo Association is a nonprofit organization of tattoo artists and enthusiasts. CTA's main goal is to share the Gospel with tattoo artists and enthusiasts. This is achieved by attending local and national tattoo conventions, developing relationships with people to provide avenues for personal witnessing, sharing their faith through the Internet and printed page, and conducting Bible studies and worship services.

National Tattoo Association

485 Business Park Lane
Allentown, PA 18109
www.nationaltattooassociation.com
email: curt@nationaltattoo.com

The National Tattoo Association was founded in 1976 with a main focus of bringing the public an awareness of tattooing as an art form. Since then, the organization has been dedicated to the advance in quality, safety standards, and professionalism in the tattooing community.

For Further Reading

Books

Kathlyn Gay and Christine Whittington, *Body Marks: Tattooing, Piercing, and Scarification.* Brookfield, CT: Millbrook, 2002. This book explores the reasons people get tattooed and pierced, the history of body art, and the controversies associated with it.

Bonnie Graves, *Tattooing and Body Piercing.* Mankato, MN: LifeMatters, 2000. This book discusses the history of tattooing and body piercing, the process of each, and the risks involved.

J.D. Lloyd, ed., *Body Piercing and Tattoos.* San Diego: Greenhaven, 2003. Through articles written by different authors, this book presents a variety of opinions regarding body piercing and tattooing. Among the issues addressed are the psychology behind permanent body art, the history of piercings and tattoos, and the potential ramifications of getting permanent body art.

Beth Wilkinson, *Coping with the Dangers of Tattooing, Body Piercing, and Scarification.* New York: Rosen, 1998. The author reviews the potential dangers of permanent body art, including health and professional issues.

Web Sites

Mayo Clinic (www.mayoclinic.com). The Mayo Clinic Web site's mission is to empower people to manage their health by providing useful and up-to-date medical information. The Web site has articles about what people should know before deciding to get pierced or tattooed, the types of infections that people can get from tattoos or piercings, and allergies that can result from certain types of jewelry used in piercings.

Tattoos, Piercing, and Body Art (http://tattoo.about.com). This site provides many links to articles about tattoos and body piercings.

University of Pennsylvania Museum of Archaeology and Anthropology (www.museum.upenn.edu). This museum has collections, exhibits, and educational programming about the world's cultural heritage. The Web site includes an online exhibit called "Bodies of Cultures" that provides information on the history and social aspects of body piercing, tattooing, and body painting.

Works Consulted

Books

Margo DeMello, *Bodies of Inscription: A Cultural History of the Modern Tattoo Community.* Durham, NC: Duke University Press, 2000. This book explores the reasons behind the rising popularity of tattooing among the middle class.

Jean-Chris Miller, *The Body Art Book: A Complete Illustrated Guide to Tattoos, Piercing, and Other Body Modifications.* New York: Berkley, 1997. Provides the basics of body art from the process of getting tattoos and body piercings to the methods for removing body art.

Victoria Pitts, *In the Flesh.* New York: Palgrave Macmillan, 2003. This work provides insight into a full range of body modification subcultures from punk rock to modern primitives.

Clinton Sanders, *Customizing the Body: The Art and Culture of Tattooing.* Philadelphia: Temple University Press, 1989. This book explores the history of tattooing, modern tattooing as an art form, and the relationship between tattooists and their clients.

V. Vale and Andrea Juno, eds., *Modern Primitives.* San Francisco: Re/Search Publications, 1989. Includes interviews with people who have practiced body art, from piercing to scarification. Those interviewed range from people famous for adorning themselves with body art to well-known tattooists and body piercers.

Periodicals

Mike McCabe, "Imagery Is Everything," *International Tattoo Art,* November 2004.

————, You Should Not Tattoo Ghosts on People," *International Tattoo Art,* November 2004.

Vaughn S. Millner and Bernard H. Eichold II, "Body Piercing and Tattooing Perspectives," *Clinical Nursing Research,* November 2001.

"Views on Tattoos," *Shape Magazine,* October 2004.

Internet Sources
Alliance of Professional Tattooists, "Frequently Asked Questions." www.safe-tattoos.com/faq.htm.

American Association of Nurse Anesthetists, "Anesthesia Risks of Tattoos and Pierced Tongues More than Skin Deep," August 26, 2004. www.aana.com/press/2004/082604.asp.

Ananova, "Leopard Man Shuns Society for Hut on Isle of Skye," 2004. www.ananova.com/news/story/sm_435810.html.

Associated Press, "Biker Told to Lose Face Tattoo or Leave Cycling Team," *Sacramento Bee,* March 1, 2005. www.sign onsandiego.com/news/state/20050301-1941-ca-cyclists tattoo.html.

——, "Tattoo Artist Stakes a Claim on Rasheed Wallace's Arm," *Detroit News,* February 15, 2005. www.detnews. com/2005/pistons/0502/15/sport-90697.htm.

BBC, "Tattoos: A Fading Craze?" March 3, 2003. www.bbc. co.uk/insideout/northwest/series2/tattoo_removal_body_art_ laser.shtml.

Charles Booth, "Now, Everybody Gets Tattoos," *Tennessean,* December 31, 2002. www.tennessean.com/local/archives/ 02/12/27100689.shtml?Element_ID=27100689.

Ann Brownfield, "Tattoos and Other Body Adornments Are More Popular than Ever, but They Still Haven't Pierced the Mainstream Business World," *Greater Milwaukee Today,* September 20, 2004. www.gmtoday.com/news/local_stories/ 2004/September_04/09202004_04.asp.

(Calcutta, India) Telegraph, "Get Set," February 25, 2005. www.telegraphindia.com/1050225/asp/calcutta/story_441958 3.asp.

Sean T. Carroll, Robert H. Riffenburgh, Timothy A. Roberts, and Elizabeth B. Myhre, "Tattoos and Body Piercings as Indicators of Adolescent Risk-Taking Behaviors," *Pediatrics,* June 2002. http://pediatrics.aappublications.org/cgi/content/full/109/6/1021.

CBC News, "Body Art: The Story Behind Tattooing and Piercing in Canada," August 30, 2004.www.cbc.ca/news/background/tattoo.

Center for Individual Freedom, "The Indelible Right of Free Expression," August 30, 2002. www.cfif.org/htdocs/freedomon line/current/in_our_opinion/tattoo_free_speech.html.

Hans H. Chen, "Tat Tactics: What Companies Think of Your Tattoos," Vault.com, 2001. www.vault.com/nr/main_article_detail.jsp?article_id=5326114&listelement=2&cat_id=0_&ht_type=5.

Justin Dickerson, "Flesh Peddling," *Macon Telegraph,* March 13, 2005. www.macon.com/mld/macon/living/11102779.htm.

R. Morgan Griffin, "All About Genital Piercing," 2003. www.bodyjewelry99.com/articles/genitalpiercing.htm.

Guardsman, "Skin Deep: Tattoo Removal," October 29, 2003. http://theguardsman.com/20031029/features.html.

Kristi L. Gustafson, "Relationship Tattoos Surge in Popularity," *Albany Times Union,* August 18, 2004. www.azcentral.com/ent/dating/articles/0818partnerart.html.

Kristopher Kaiyala, "The Skin Game: Once 'Graffiti,' Now Body Art," MSNBC.com, November 2, 2004. www.msnbc.msn.com/id/6124648.

Marisa Kakoulas, "The Tattoo Copyright Controversy," *Body Modification Ezine,* December 8, 2003. www.bmezine.com/news/guest/20031208.html.

Lisa Klassen, "A Piece of Art," *Daily Bruin,* February 6, 2001. www.dailybruin.ucla.edu/db/printer.asp?ID=2790.

Shannon Larratt, "BME Commentary on PA House Bill No. 615," *Body Modification Ezine,* November 9, 2004. www.bmezine.com/news/pubring/20041109.html.

————, "Regulation: Attacks from Within?" *Body Modification Ezine,* June 15, 2003. www.bmezine.com/news/pubring/20030615.html.

————, "Tongue Splitting FAQ," *Body Modification Ezine,* May 27, 2003. www.bmezine.com/tsplitfaq.html.

Matt Leingang, "Two Teens Ill After Tattoos," *Cincinnati Enquirer,* May 8, 2004. www.enquirer.com/editions/2004/05/08/loc_illegaltattoo.html.

Hoag Levins, "The Changing Cultural Status of Tattoo Art," 1998. www.tattooartist.com/history.html.

Kelly Luker, "Needle Freaks," *Metro,* July 26–August 1, 2001. www.metroactive.com/papers/metro/07.26.01/cover/tattoo-0130.html.

J. Frank Lynch, "Fayette Policy on Body Piercings Less Strict than Henry," *(Fayette, Georgia) Citizen,* October 13, 2004. www.thecitizennews.com/main/archive-041013/in-04.htm.

Andres Martin, "On Teenagers and Tattoos (Tattoos Signify Belonging or a Sense of Permanence to Teenagers)," *Journal of the American Academy of Child and Adolescent Psychiatry,* June 1997. www.findarticles.com/p/articles/mi_hb179/is_199706/ai_n5572459.

MSNBC, "Eyeball Jewelry—a New Dutch Fashion Trend," April 7, 2004. www.msnbc.msn.com/id/4685961.

————, "The Risks of Do-It-Yourself Tattoos," February 25, 2004. www.msnbc.msn.com/id/4370500.

Lauralee Ortiz, "Permanent Makeup: Tattoo Technique 'Looks Natural and Saves an Awful Lot of Time,'" *Detroit Free Press,* February 10, 2004. www.facialart.net/Free%20Press%20Feb04.htm.

Painful Pleasures, "Body Piercing History." www.painfulpleasures.com/piercing_history.htm.

Dick Patrick, "Body Piercing Penetrates Athletes," *USA Today,* October 20, 1999. http//pqasb.pqarchiver.com/USAToday/

45697041.html?did=45697041&FMT=ABS&FMTS=FT&
date=Oct+20%2C+1999&author=Dick+Patrick&desc=Body+
piercing+penetrates+athletics.

Peggy Peck, "Thinking About Getting a Tattoo? Think Again,"
WebMD, April 9, 2001. http://my.webmd.com/content/article/
35/1728_76844.htm.

Tom Rickey, "Teens, Body Piercing, and Risky Behavior Go
Together," *UniSci,* May 7, 2002. http://unisci.com/stories/
20022/0507024.htm.

Kelly Rothenberg, "Tattooed People as Taboo Figures in
Modern Society," 1996. www.bmezine.com/tattoo/tattab.html.

John Schneider, "Woman with Skull Is 'Tattoo Tale' Winner,"
Lansing State Journal, July 30, 2004.www.lsj.com/news/
capitol/040730_john_lb.html.

Science a GoGo, "Risks of Body Piercing to People with
Heart Conditions," June 8, 1999. www.scienceagogo.com/
news/19990507210109data_trunc_sys.shtml.

Steel Navel, "SteelNavel.com News," January 2002. www.steel
navel.com/news/body-jewelry-news-02-1.asp.

Travis Swink, "Local Tattoo Artists Push for Health Standards,"
Northwest Trail Online. http://trail.nwc.cc.wy.us/Trail%20Extra/
17tattoo.html.

Mark Washofsky, "Cosmetic Surgery: A Jewish View," My
JewishLearning.com. www.myjewishlearning.com/daily_life/
TheBody/Adorning_the_Body/Cosmetic_Surgery.htm.

Caoimhe Young, "A Passion for Piercing; 'Our Clients Range
from Teenagers to Teachers,'" *(London) Sunday Mirror,*
September 27, 1998. http://static.highbeam.com/s/sunday
mirrorlondonengland/september271998/apassionforpiercing
ourclientsrangefromteenagerstot.

Yasmine Zaki, "Nipple Accessories—Strange or Trendy?"
Daily Helmsman, February 17, 2004. www.dailyhelmsman.
com/vnews/display.v/ART/2004/02/17/4031a28c33a2e.

Index

Picture Credits

About the Author

Leanne K. Currie-McGhee's articles and stories have appeared in *Pockets, My Friend, Guideposts for Kids,* and *Highlights for Children.* She is also the author of *Gun Control* and *Animal Rights,* both published by Lucent Books. Ms. Currie-McGhee resides in Norfolk, Virginia, with her husband, Keith, and daughter, Grace.